Strategic Procurement and Supply Chain Management

A Professional's Guide

Table of Contents
Strategic Procurement and Supply Chain Management
A Professional's Guide

Purpose of the Book	**5**
Part 1: Fundamentals of Procurement and Supply Chain Management	**9**
Chapter 1: Introduction to Supply Chain Management	**10**
The Evolution of Supply Chain Management	14
Chapter 2: Basics of Procurement	**20**
Definition and Importance of Procurement	21
Types of Procurement: Direct, Indirect, and Strategic Procurement	25
Procurement vs. Purchasing	30
Chapter 3: Supply Chain Models and Frameworks SCOR	**37**
SCOR (Supply Chain Operations Reference) Model	38
Lean and Agile Supply Chain Concepts	45
The Bullwhip Effect and its implications	51
Part 2: Strategic Procurement Chapter	**57**
4: Procurement Planning	**58**
Developing procurement strategies aligned with business objectives.	59
Category Management and Spend Analysis	64
Make-or-Buy Decisions	70
Chapter 5: Supplier Selection and Evaluation	**77**
Criteria for Supplier Selection	78
Vendor Evaluation Tools: RFI, RFQ, and RFP	82
Supplier Performance Management	88
Chapter 6: Strategic Sourcing	**95**
Strategic Sourcing: Definition and Process	96
Total Cost of Ownership (TCO)	102
Risk Management in Sourcing	108
Chapter 7: Negotiation and Contract Management	**115**
Principles of Effective Negotiation	116
Types of Procurement Contracts	121
Contract Lifecycle Management	126
Part 3: Advanced Supply Chain Management	**132**
Chapter 8: Demand Planning and Forecasting	**133**

Role of Demand Planning in the Supply Chain	134
Forecasting Methods: Quantitative and Qualitative Approaches	139
Collaborative Forecasting Techniques	145

Chapter 9: Inventory Management and Optimization — 152
- Types of Inventory and Their Roles — 153
- Techniques for Inventory Control (EOQ, Safety Stock) — 158
- Inventory Optimization in Supply Chains — 163

Chapter 10: Logistics and Distribution Management — 170
- Transportation Modes and Selection Criteria — 171
- Warehousing and Distribution Strategies — 178
- Cross-docking and Last-Mile Delivery — 184

Chapter 11: Technology in Supply Chain Management — 191
- Role of ERP and supply chain software. — 192
- Impact of IoT, AI, and Blockchain on Supply Chains — 198

Part 4: Sustainable and Resilient Supply Chains — 205

Chapter 12: Sustainable Procurement — 206
- Green Procurement Strategies — 207
- Environmental and Social Governance (ESG) in Procurement — 210
- Circular Supply Chain Concepts — 213

Chapter 13: Building Resilient Supply Chains — 220
- Managing Disruptions and Risks — 221
- Strategies for Supply Chain Resilience — 223
- Case Studies on Successful Resilience Practices — 227

Part 5: Procurement and Supply Chain Leadership — 233

Chapter 14: Leadership in Procurement and Supply Chain — 234
- Skills for Modern Procurement and Supply Chain Leaders — 235
- Collaboration Across Teams and Departments — 238
- Leadership Case Studies in Procurement and Supply Chain Management — 240

Chapter 15: Performance Measurement — 248
- Key Performance Indicators (KPIs) for Procurement and Supply Chain — 249
- Balanced Scorecard Approach — 252

4. Learning & Growth Perspective — 254
- Continuous improvement frameworks. — 255

Chapter 16: Future Trends in Procurement and Supply Chain Management — 262
- The Rise of Automation and Autonomous Systems — 263

Evolving Global Trade Dynamics	265
Predictions for the Next Decade in Procurement and Supply Chain Management	267
Conclusion	**273**
Recap of Key Lessons	273
Call to Action for Professionals to Apply Strategies Effectively	274
Additional Resources	**275**
Templates for Procurement and Supply Chain Management	278
Recommended Reading and References	279
Appendix	**282**

Purpose of the Book

Importance of Procurement and Supply Chain Management in Modern Business

In today's fast-paced, interconnected world, procurement and supply chain management play pivotal roles in shaping the success and resilience of organizations. The importance of these functions cannot be overstated, as they form the backbone of operations, enabling companies to deliver products and services efficiently, cost-effectively, and sustainably. Whether in manufacturing, retail, healthcare, or technology, the strategic management of procurement and supply chains directly impacts profitability, competitiveness, and customer satisfaction.

Procurement, often perceived as a routine transactional activity, has evolved into a strategic function that influences every aspect of an organization. It is no longer about merely acquiring goods and services at the lowest cost; instead, it encompasses supplier relationship management, risk mitigation, and value creation. Effective procurement ensures that organizations have access to high-quality materials and services, fostering innovation and operational excellence. It also enables businesses to navigate the complexities of global markets, where factors like fluctuating commodity prices, geopolitical tensions, and environmental concerns challenge traditional procurement models.

Supply chain management, on the other hand, is the art and science of optimizing the flow of goods, information, and finances from the point of origin to the point of consumption. In a globalized economy, supply chains have become highly intricate networks involving multiple stakeholders, from suppliers and manufacturers to distributors and customers. The ability to manage these networks effectively determines a company's ability to meet customer demands, maintain inventory levels, and respond to disruptions. Organizations with robust supply chain strategies can reduce lead times, lower costs, and improve service levels, gaining a competitive edge in their industries.

The COVID-19 pandemic underscored the critical importance of procurement and supply chain management. As businesses faced unprecedented disruptions—from factory closures and transportation bottlenecks to skyrocketing demand for essential goods—it became evident that supply chains are not merely operational necessities but strategic assets. Companies that had invested in resilient, agile supply chains were better equipped to weather the storm, highlighting the need for proactive and strategic management.

Moreover, the growing emphasis on sustainability has elevated the role of procurement and supply chain management. Businesses are under increasing pressure from consumers, regulators, and investors to adopt environmentally and socially responsible practices. Sustainable procurement involves sourcing materials and services in ways that minimize environmental impact, uphold ethical labor practices, and support local communities. Similarly, sustainable supply chains prioritize renewable resources, waste reduction, and circular economy principles, ensuring long-term viability and positive societal impact.

Overview of the Book Structure

This book is designed as a comprehensive guide for professionals seeking to deepen their understanding of procurement and supply chain management. It combines theoretical insights with practical applications, offering readers a holistic perspective on these interconnected disciplines. The content is organized into logical sections, each addressing a critical aspect of procurement and supply chain management, to provide a well-rounded learning experience.

The initial chapters focus on foundational concepts, setting the stage for more advanced topics. These chapters explore the evolution of procurement and supply chain management, highlighting the transition from traditional operational roles to strategic enablers of business success. By understanding the historical context and current trends, readers will appreciate the dynamic nature of these fields and their relevance in modern business.

Subsequent chapters delve into strategic procurement, covering topics such as supplier selection, contract management, and negotiation. These chapters emphasize the importance of aligning procurement strategies with organizational goals, fostering collaborative partnerships, and leveraging technology for efficiency. Readers will gain insights into best practices for managing complex supplier networks, mitigating risks, and achieving cost savings without compromising quality.

The book then transitions to advanced supply chain management, addressing areas such as demand planning, inventory optimization, logistics, and distribution. These chapters provide actionable frameworks and tools for managing the intricate web of supply chain activities, ensuring seamless operations and customer satisfaction. Real-world examples and case studies illustrate how successful organizations have overcome challenges and capitalized on opportunities, offering valuable lessons for professionals.

Recognizing the growing significance of sustainability and resilience, the book dedicates sections to these critical themes. It explores strategies for integrating environmental, social, and governance (ESG) considerations into procurement and supply chain decisions, as well as approaches for building robust, adaptable supply chains capable of withstanding disruptions. These chapters encourage readers to think beyond short-term gains, emphasizing the importance of long-term value creation and risk management.

Leadership and performance measurement are also central to the book's narrative. As procurement and supply chain management become increasingly strategic, the need for effective leadership and robust performance metrics becomes paramount. The book provides guidance on developing leadership skills, fostering cross-functional collaboration, and implementing key performance indicators (KPIs) to drive continuous improvement.

The final chapters explore emerging trends and future directions in procurement and supply chain management. Topics such as digital transformation, automation, and globalization are examined in depth, equipping readers with the knowledge to navigate an ever-changing landscape. By understanding these trends, professionals can position themselves and their organizations for success in a highly competitive environment.

This book is not merely a theoretical treatise but a practical resource for professionals at all levels. Whether you are a seasoned supply chain manager, a procurement specialist, or a business leader seeking to enhance operational efficiency, this book offers valuable insights and actionable strategies. It combines in-depth analysis with clear explanations, ensuring accessibility without sacrificing rigor.

Through its structured approach, the book aims to empower professionals to excel in their roles, contribute to organizational success, and drive meaningful change in the field of procurement and supply chain management. By bridging the gap between theory and practice, it aspires to be a trusted companion for those navigating the complexities of modern business.

Part 1: Fundamentals of Procurement and Supply Chain Management

Chapter 1: Introduction to Supply Chain Management

Definition of Supply Chain Management

Supply Chain Management (SCM) is a comprehensive and strategic approach to managing the flow of goods, services, information, and finances from the origin of raw materials to the final delivery of finished products to customers. It involves coordinating and integrating these flows within and across companies to create value, reduce costs, and meet customer demands efficiently.

At its core, supply chain management seeks to optimize the interconnected network of suppliers, manufacturers, warehouses, distribution centers, and retailers. This optimization ensures that products are delivered to the right place, at the right time, in the right quantity, and at the right cost. SCM transcends individual organizational boundaries and requires collaboration across the entire network to achieve shared objectives.

In a globalized and highly competitive business environment, the significance of SCM has grown exponentially. Organizations that can efficiently manage their supply chains gain a competitive advantage by reducing costs, enhancing customer satisfaction, and increasing operational resilience. Moreover, the integration of technology and data analytics has transformed SCM into a dynamic and data-driven discipline, enabling organizations to anticipate and respond to market changes effectively.

Components of the Supply Chain

The supply chain comprises several interdependent components, each playing a critical role in ensuring the smooth flow of goods and services. These components work together as a cohesive system, and any disruption in one area can have ripple effects throughout the chain. The primary components of a supply chain include:

1. Suppliers

Suppliers are the starting point of the supply chain. They provide the raw materials, components, and services required for production. Effective supplier management involves selecting reliable suppliers, establishing long-term relationships, and ensuring consistent quality and timely delivery. Strategic sourcing and supplier performance evaluation are essential to mitigate risks and maintain a seamless supply chain.

2. Manufacturers

Manufacturers transform raw materials and components into finished products through various production processes. This stage involves production planning, scheduling, and quality control to ensure that products meet customer expectations and adhere to regulatory standards. Manufacturers must balance efficiency with flexibility to adapt to changing demand and minimize waste.

3. Warehouses and Storage Facilities

Warehouses play a crucial role in storing raw materials, semi-finished goods, and finished products. Effective warehousing ensures the availability of products when needed, reduces lead times, and minimizes inventory holding costs. Modern warehouses often utilize advanced technologies, such as automated storage and retrieval systems (AS/RS), to improve efficiency and accuracy.

4. Distribution Centers

Distribution centers act as hubs for sorting, packaging, and redistributing products to various destinations. They bridge the gap between manufacturers and retailers or end customers. Efficient distribution strategies, including cross-docking and just-in-time delivery, are essential to reduce costs and enhance customer satisfaction.

5. Transportation

Transportation is the lifeline of the supply chain, facilitating the movement of goods from one point to another. It encompasses various modes, such as road, rail, air, and sea, each with its advantages and limitations. Choosing the right transportation mode and optimizing routes are critical for cost efficiency and timely delivery.

6. Retailers and Distributors
Retailers and distributors act as intermediaries between manufacturers and end consumers. They ensure that products are available to customers in the right quantities and locations. Retailers play a key role in demand forecasting and customer relationship management, while distributors focus on logistics and inventory management.

7. Customers
Customers are the ultimate focus of the supply chain. Understanding and meeting customer needs drive all supply chain activities. Organizations must prioritize customer satisfaction by delivering high-quality products, ensuring on-time delivery, and providing excellent after-sales service.

8. Information Flow
Information is the glue that binds all supply chain components together. Accurate and timely information exchange is essential for effective decision-making, demand forecasting, and inventory management. Advanced technologies, such as Enterprise Resource Planning (ERP) systems and blockchain, enable real-time data sharing and enhance transparency across the supply chain.

9. Financial Flow
Financial flow refers to the movement of funds across the supply chain, including payments to suppliers, operational expenses, and revenue collection from customers. Efficient financial management ensures cash flow stability and reduces the cost of capital.

10. Reverse Logistics
Reverse logistics involves the return of goods from customers to the manufacturer or supplier for repair, recycling, or disposal. This component is increasingly important in the context of sustainability and circular economy practices, as organizations strive to minimize waste and maximize resource utilization.

By understanding the definition and components of the supply chain, professionals can appreciate the complexity and interdependence of supply chain activities. Effective supply chain management requires a holistic approach that considers each component's role and optimizes the entire network for seamless operations and value creation. This foundational knowledge sets the stage for exploring advanced concepts and strategies in procurement and supply chain management.

The Evolution of Supply Chain Management

Supply chain management (SCM) is a concept that has undergone significant transformation over the centuries, evolving from basic trade and bartering systems to complex, interconnected global networks. This progression has been driven by advancements in technology, shifts in market demands, globalization, and a growing emphasis on sustainability and efficiency. Understanding the evolution of supply chain management provides valuable context for its current practices and highlights the factors shaping its future trajectory.

The Early Foundations of Supply Chain Management

The roots of supply chain management can be traced back to ancient times when societies relied on rudimentary systems of trade and logistics. Early civilizations such as Mesopotamia, Egypt, and the Indus Valley developed basic supply chains to facilitate trade, agriculture, and the distribution of resources.

These early supply chains were characterized by localized production and consumption. Bartering systems were the primary mode of exchange, with communities trading goods and services directly. Infrastructure development, such as roads, waterways, and storage facilities, played a pivotal role in expanding trade networks and improving the flow of goods.

In ancient Egypt, for example, the construction of the pyramids required highly organized supply chains to transport massive quantities of limestone, granite, and food supplies. Similarly, the Silk Road, an extensive trade network connecting Asia, Europe, and Africa, exemplified the importance of logistics in enabling cross-regional commerce.

The Industrial Revolution and the Rise of Manufacturing

The Industrial Revolution in the 18th and 19th centuries marked a significant turning point in the evolution of supply chain management. The advent of mechanization and mass production transformed supply chains from localized, manual systems into more structured and scalable operations.
Factories became central to production, and supply chains expanded to include suppliers, manufacturers, and distributors. The introduction of steam-powered transportation, such as railways and steamships, facilitated faster and more cost-effective movement of goods over long distances.

Standardization of production processes and the development of assembly lines, pioneered by innovators like Henry Ford, further enhanced efficiency and reduced production costs. This era saw the emergence of supply chain concepts such as inventory management, distribution planning, and procurement strategies.

The Post-World War II Era: Integration and Efficiency

The period following World War II witnessed rapid advancements in technology and globalization, which significantly influenced supply chain practices. As economies recovered and international trade flourished, businesses began to focus on integrating supply chain functions to achieve greater efficiency and cost savings.

The introduction of containerization revolutionized shipping by standardizing cargo handling, reducing transportation costs, and improving reliability. This innovation enabled the seamless movement of goods across multiple modes of transport, such as ships, trucks, and trains.

During this era, concepts such as Just-in-Time (JIT) manufacturing, popularized by Toyota, gained prominence. JIT emphasized reducing inventory levels by producing goods only when needed, thereby minimizing waste and improving responsiveness to customer demands.

The development of information technology, particularly in the 1980s, paved the way for computer-based inventory management systems and Enterprise Resource Planning (ERP) software. These tools enabled organizations to streamline their supply chain operations, enhance visibility, and improve decision-making.

The Globalization of Supply Chains

The late 20th century saw the globalization of supply chains as companies sought to leverage cost advantages, access new markets, and diversify their operations. Outsourcing and offshoring became prevalent, with businesses establishing manufacturing facilities and sourcing materials from low-cost regions such as China, India, and Southeast Asia.

Global supply chains introduced new complexities, including extended lead times, cultural differences, and geopolitical risks. However, they also offered opportunities for economies of scale, increased competitiveness, and access to a broader talent pool.

Technological advancements in telecommunications, such as the internet and satellite communication, facilitated real-time tracking and coordination across global supply chains. Companies began to adopt supply chain management strategies that emphasized collaboration, risk management, and sustainability.

The Digital Revolution and the Rise of Technology

The 21st century ushered in the digital revolution, which has fundamentally reshaped supply chain management. Technologies such as artificial intelligence (AI), blockchain, the Internet of Things (IoT), and big data analytics have enabled unprecedented levels of visibility, automation, and efficiency.

IoT devices allow for real-time tracking of goods, providing critical insights into inventory levels, shipment status, and environmental conditions. Blockchain technology enhances transparency and trust by creating immutable records of transactions and ensuring the authenticity of goods.

AI and machine learning algorithms are increasingly used for demand forecasting, route optimization, and predictive maintenance. These technologies enable supply chains to be more agile and responsive to changes in demand and supply conditions.

E-commerce giants like Amazon have set new benchmarks for supply chain excellence by leveraging robotics, automated fulfillment centers, and data-driven decision-making. The rise of omni-channel retailing has further emphasized the need for seamless integration of online and offline supply chain operations.

The Shift Towards Sustainability

In recent years, sustainability has become a central theme in supply chain management. Companies are under increasing pressure from stakeholders, regulators, and consumers to adopt environmentally and socially responsible practices.
Sustainable supply chains prioritize reducing carbon emissions, minimizing waste, and sourcing materials ethically. Strategies such as circular supply chains, green logistics, and renewable energy integration are gaining traction as businesses strive to meet sustainability goals while maintaining profitability.

Governments and industry bodies are also introducing regulations to promote sustainability, such as carbon pricing and extended producer responsibility (EPR) laws. Companies that proactively address these challenges can gain a competitive advantage and enhance their brand reputation.

The Impact of Global Disruptions

The COVID-19 pandemic highlighted the vulnerabilities of global supply chains, such as dependence on single sources, lack of resilience, and inadequate risk management strategies. The crisis underscored the importance of building agile and adaptable supply chains that can withstand disruptions.

In response, businesses are re-evaluating their supply chain strategies, focusing on diversification, digital transformation, and local sourcing. Resilience has become a key priority, with companies investing in technologies that enhance visibility, scenario planning, and risk mitigation.

The Future of Supply Chain Management

As supply chains continue to evolve, several trends are shaping their future. These include:

- The adoption of autonomous vehicles and drones for last-mile delivery.

- The integration of renewable energy sources and sustainable materials.

- The use of digital twins for real-time simulation and optimization of supply chain operations.

- Increased collaboration between stakeholders through digital platforms and ecosystems.

The evolution of supply chain management is a testament to human ingenuity and adaptability. From its humble beginnings in ancient trade networks to the sophisticated, technology-driven systems of today, SCM has continually adapted to meet the needs of businesses and society. By embracing innovation and prioritizing sustainability, supply chain professionals can navigate the complexities of the modern world and drive value for all stakeholders.

Chapter 2: Basics of Procurement

Definition and Importance of Procurement

Procurement is a fundamental aspect of business operations that refers to the process of acquiring goods, services, or works from external sources. This process is essential for organizations to obtain the necessary resources to carry out their day-to-day functions, meet customer demands, and maintain competitive advantage. Procurement involves identifying needs, selecting suppliers, negotiating contracts, and managing relationships to ensure the timely and cost-effective delivery of quality products and services.

In the broader context of supply chain management, procurement plays a central role in sourcing inputs and ensuring that all components of the supply chain operate smoothly. It is not just about purchasing goods at the lowest price, but rather about obtaining the right goods, at the right price, at the right time, and from the right sources. Effective procurement is a strategic activity that helps organizations reduce costs, mitigate risks, and enhance operational performance.

Procurement is often categorized into two main areas: direct procurement and indirect procurement. Direct procurement refers to the acquisition of goods or services that are directly involved in the production process, such as raw materials, components, and machinery. Indirect procurement, on the other hand, covers non-production-related items such as office supplies, IT services, and maintenance contracts.

Procurement is more than just a transactional activity; it requires strategic thinking, market analysis, negotiation skills, and relationship management. It involves coordination with various stakeholders, including internal departments (such as finance, operations, and logistics) and external suppliers. Procurement professionals need to possess strong decision-making abilities, as they play a crucial role in determining the quality, cost, and availability of resources required for organizational success.

The importance of procurement cannot be overstated. It is a function that directly impacts a company's bottom line and operational efficiency. By sourcing high-quality goods and services at competitive prices, procurement professionals can help organizations minimize costs, optimize resources, and increase profitability. Furthermore, procurement is integral to mitigating supply chain risks, as it enables businesses to diversify their supplier base, reduce reliance on single sources, and ensure supply continuity.

Procurement also plays a key role in fostering innovation and creating long-term value for organizations. By working closely with suppliers, procurement teams can identify opportunities for collaboration, product improvement, and innovation. Effective supplier relationship management is essential for ensuring that both parties are aligned in their goals, and that suppliers are committed to delivering value beyond the basic contractual terms.

Moreover, procurement is increasingly seen as a strategic function, contributing to the overall goals and objectives of the organization. In today's competitive business environment, companies must focus on securing a reliable supply of high-quality goods and services that are both cost-effective and sustainable. With growing concerns about environmental impact and social responsibility, procurement is also becoming a key driver of corporate social responsibility (CSR) initiatives. Many organizations are now prioritizing ethical sourcing, sustainability, and supplier diversity as part of their procurement strategies.

Key Objectives of Procurement

The primary objectives of procurement are to secure the necessary resources for the business, ensure timely delivery, and minimize costs while maintaining quality standards. The key objectives can be broken down into several components:

Cost Efficiency: One of the main goals of procurement is to source goods and services at the most competitive prices. However, cost efficiency does not mean choosing the lowest price. Instead, procurement professionals aim to strike a balance between price, quality, and value. Through effective negotiation, supplier selection, and strategic sourcing, procurement can help organizations optimize their spending.

Quality Assurance: Procurement is responsible for ensuring that the goods and services purchased meet the required standards and specifications. Quality assurance is essential to prevent defects, reduce waste, and enhance the overall product or service output. Procurement teams often collaborate with suppliers to define quality standards, establish inspection processes, and implement testing procedures to ensure compliance.

Timeliness and Reliability: Ensuring that products and services are delivered on time is a critical aspect of procurement. Delays in procurement can disrupt operations, cause production downtime, and negatively affect customer satisfaction. Therefore, procurement teams must work with suppliers to establish clear delivery timelines, monitor progress, and take corrective actions when necessary.

Risk Management: The procurement process also involves assessing and mitigating risks related to supply chain disruptions, market fluctuations, geopolitical factors, and supplier reliability. Procurement professionals need to diversify suppliers, develop contingency plans, and ensure that contracts include risk mitigation clauses to protect the organization from unforeseen events.

Supplier Relationship Management: Building strong, long-term relationships with suppliers is crucial to successful procurement. By fostering trust, open communication, and collaboration, procurement professionals can develop mutually beneficial partnerships that lead to better pricing, improved service, and innovation. Supplier relationship management goes beyond transactional exchanges and focuses on creating value through cooperation and shared goals.

Sustainability and Ethical Sourcing: In recent years, procurement has increasingly become a vehicle for promoting sustainability and ethical business practices. Many organizations are prioritizing environmentally friendly sourcing and selecting suppliers who adhere to ethical labor practices, human rights standards, and fair trade principles. Procurement teams are now tasked with ensuring that suppliers align with the company's values and sustainability goals.

Procurement in the Global Context

With the rise of globalization, procurement has become more complex and far-reaching. Companies are now sourcing materials and services from all corners of the globe, and the challenges associated with managing international procurement have grown significantly. Factors such as currency fluctuations, customs regulations, political instability, and cultural differences must be carefully considered when sourcing globally.

Global procurement offers opportunities for cost savings and access to a broader range of suppliers, but it also introduces risks such as longer lead times, supply chain disruptions, and difficulty in monitoring supplier compliance. Therefore, procurement professionals must be equipped with the tools and knowledge to manage the intricacies of global sourcing, including international logistics, trade regulations, and geopolitical risks.

In response to these challenges, many organizations are adopting technology-driven solutions such as digital procurement platforms, cloud-based supply chain management tools, and artificial intelligence (AI) to streamline procurement processes and enhance decision-making capabilities. These innovations are enabling procurement teams to improve efficiency, reduce errors, and gain deeper insights into supplier performance, market trends, and supply chain risks.

Procurement is a vital function that influences the operational and financial performance of an organization. It is responsible for acquiring the resources necessary for day-to-day operations, and its impact extends across all aspects of business, from production to customer satisfaction. Effective procurement not only ensures cost efficiency and quality but also plays a key role in mitigating risks, fostering innovation, and driving sustainability. As businesses continue to operate in an increasingly globalized and digital environment, procurement will remain an essential function in achieving organizational success and maintaining a competitive edge.

Types of Procurement: Direct, Indirect, and Strategic Procurement

Procurement is a crucial business function that encompasses the sourcing and acquisition of goods and services necessary for a company's operations. Understanding the different types of procurement is essential for professionals in the field, as it enables organizations to allocate resources effectively, optimize processes, and manage relationships with suppliers. While procurement strategies can vary significantly depending on the specific needs of a business, the three main types of procurement—direct, indirect, and strategic procurement—play distinct roles in shaping an organization's overall procurement strategy.

Direct Procurement

Direct procurement, also referred to as "production procurement" or "core procurement," involves the sourcing of goods and services that are directly tied to an organization's production process. These are the essential materials, components, and supplies needed for the creation of the company's primary products or services.

In manufacturing industries, direct procurement typically includes raw materials, semi-finished goods, and components required to produce finished products. For example, in the automotive industry, direct procurement would involve the acquisition of metals, engines, tires, and other parts that are incorporated into vehicles during the production process. Similarly, for a food manufacturer, direct procurement would include ingredients like flour, sugar, and vegetables, which are used in the final products.

Direct procurement is crucial because it directly impacts the quality, cost, and timeliness of production. By securing high-quality materials at competitive prices, businesses can maintain production efficiency, avoid costly delays, and meet customer demand. Additionally, direct procurement often involves long-term contracts and close relationships with suppliers to ensure consistent delivery of high-quality inputs.

Key Characteristics of Direct Procurement:

Direct impact on product manufacturing: The procured items are essential to the production process and end product.

Focus on quality and consistency: Companies often develop long-term relationships with suppliers to ensure stable and reliable supply chains.

Volume-based contracts: Direct procurement typically involves large volumes, requiring detailed forecasting, order management, and cost control.

Indirect Procurement

Indirect procurement, in contrast to direct procurement, refers to the acquisition of goods and services that are not directly involved in the production of a company's products or services but are necessary for the overall functioning of the business. These items are often referred to as "non-production goods" or "operational supplies."

Examples of indirect procurement include office supplies (such as computers, stationery, and furniture), IT services, maintenance and repair services, professional services (such as consulting and legal services), and utilities like electricity and water. Indirect procurement also covers services that support the core business operations, including marketing services, employee training, and travel expenses.

While indirect procurement may not be directly tied to the production process, it plays a critical role in ensuring the smooth operation of the organization. Efficient indirect procurement can help businesses reduce operational costs, improve organizational productivity, and ensure that the necessary infrastructure and resources are in place to support core activities.

Key Characteristics of Indirect Procurement:

Supportive role: Indirect procurement supports the overall functioning of the organization rather than directly contributing to the production of goods or services.

Diverse and fragmented: Indirect procurement typically involves a wide variety of goods and services, many of which can be sourced from different suppliers.

Operational efficiency: Cost reduction and streamlining operations are key goals in managing indirect procurement, often through consolidated contracts and strategic sourcing.

Strategic Procurement

Strategic procurement is a more advanced and proactive approach that aligns procurement activities with the long-term objectives of the organization. This type of procurement goes beyond day-to-day sourcing and purchasing and involves a focus on optimizing the procurement process in the context of broader business goals. Strategic procurement is about creating value through supplier partnerships, risk management, and continuous improvement, ensuring that procurement decisions align with the organization's overall strategy and competitive advantage.

Strategic procurement involves several key components:

Supplier Relationship Management (SRM): Strategic procurement emphasizes building long-term, collaborative relationships with key suppliers. By managing these relationships strategically, companies can ensure that their suppliers are aligned with their business needs, share in innovation, and contribute to cost savings, quality improvements, and risk mitigation.

Total Cost of Ownership (TCO): Instead of focusing solely on the purchase price of goods or services, strategic procurement considers the total cost of ownership. This includes direct costs (like purchase price) and indirect costs (such as maintenance, training, and disposal). By understanding TCO, procurement professionals can make more informed decisions and select suppliers who offer the best overall value.

Category Management: This approach involves grouping procurement activities by categories (e.g., IT, logistics, raw materials) and focusing on strategic sourcing and supplier management within each category. By consolidating procurement activities into well-defined categories, organizations can leverage economies of scale, standardize processes, and drive greater value from suppliers.

Sustainability and Risk Management: Strategic procurement involves considering environmental, social, and governance (ESG) factors when making sourcing decisions. As sustainability becomes a critical focus for businesses, procurement professionals are tasked with finding suppliers who share the company's commitment to ethical practices, environmental responsibility, and social impact. In addition, risk management plays a significant role, with strategic procurement professionals assessing and mitigating risks that could affect supply chains, such as geopolitical instability or natural disasters.

Key Characteristics of Strategic Procurement:

Alignment with organizational strategy: Strategic procurement focuses on long-term objectives, such as cost reduction, innovation, and competitive advantage.

Collaboration and partnerships: Building strong supplier relationships is a cornerstone of strategic procurement, enabling collaboration and joint problem-solving.

Continuous improvement: Strategic procurement seeks to improve the procurement process, supplier performance, and value creation over time.

Proactive approach: Unlike reactive procurement, which focuses on immediate needs, strategic procurement anticipates future needs and prepares for market changes.

Comparison of Direct, Indirect, and Strategic Procurement

Each type of procurement serves a unique purpose within an organization, and understanding the differences between direct, indirect, and strategic procurement is essential for procurement professionals. The key distinctions lie in the scope of goods and services acquired, the impact on the organization, and the level of collaboration with suppliers.

Direct Procurement is focused on the immediate needs of production and manufacturing. It is highly transactional and requires an efficient process to secure essential materials, components, and services.

Indirect Procurement supports the overall functioning of the organization by sourcing non-production goods and services, which are critical for business operations but do not directly contribute to the end product.

Strategic Procurement takes a long-term, holistic view of procurement. It is focused on optimizing procurement activities to create value, foster supplier relationships, and align procurement decisions with the overall goals of the organization.

While direct and indirect procurement are often more transactional, strategic procurement requires a deeper understanding of the organization's goals, a focus on long-term relationships with suppliers, and the ability to navigate complex issues such as sustainability and risk management.

Understanding the various types of procurement is vital for procurement professionals in managing their responsibilities and contributing to the overall success of an organization. Direct procurement ensures the smooth flow of materials necessary for production, while indirect procurement supports organizational operations. Strategic procurement, on the other hand, focuses on adding value through supplier collaboration, innovation, and risk management. By recognizing the distinct roles these procurement types play and aligning them with the broader business strategy, organizations can optimize procurement processes, reduce costs, and improve their competitive edge.

Procurement vs. Purchasing

The terms **procurement** and **purchasing** are often used interchangeably in business settings, but they represent distinct concepts, especially in the context of supply chain management. Both are essential functions within an organization, but they differ in scope, objectives, and overall impact. Understanding the differences between procurement and purchasing is vital for professionals seeking to optimize their sourcing processes, streamline operations, and add value to the business.

Defining Procurement

Procurement is a strategic process that involves the entire cycle of acquiring goods and services from external suppliers. It is much broader than purchasing and covers various activities beyond just the transaction of buying goods. Procurement encompasses everything from identifying business needs to selecting suppliers, negotiating contracts, managing supplier relationships, and ensuring that the acquired goods or services meet the organization's quality standards, timelines, and budget.

Procurement involves both **strategic** and **operational** elements. It includes activities such as:

Identifying the organization's needs and requirements.

Conducting market research to find potential suppliers.

Managing relationships with suppliers to ensure long-term value and reliability.

Evaluating supplier performance and fostering continuous improvement.

Negotiating contracts, including terms, pricing, and delivery schedules.

Managing risks, compliance, and sustainability practices within the supply chain.

The ultimate goal of procurement is to ensure that the organization is obtaining the best possible value from its suppliers while aligning purchases with its overall business objectives, such as cost reduction, innovation, and quality enhancement. Procurement is a **strategic function** that often influences the direction of business operations by aligning with corporate goals and objectives.

Defining Purchasing

Purchasing, on the other hand, is a subset of procurement. It refers to the transactional aspect of acquiring goods or services that an organization needs. Purchasing is the act of ordering and receiving goods, which is generally viewed as a more tactical function that focuses on the physical exchange of goods or services for payment. The purchasing process involves:

Issuing purchase orders based on identified needs.

Receiving and inspecting goods or services.

Ensuring timely payment to suppliers.

Managing inventory and ensuring the smooth flow of goods into the organization.

While purchasing is concerned primarily with the buying process itself, it is often viewed as a **reactive function** that responds to immediate requirements. Purchasing decisions are typically guided by **pre-determined specifications**, and it focuses more on ensuring the right items are acquired at the right time and at the right price.

Key Differences Between Procurement and Purchasing

Scope and Focus

Procurement is a comprehensive process that includes planning, supplier relationship management, contract negotiation, risk management, and long-term value creation.

It is more strategic in nature, focusing on the broader goals of the organization.

Purchasing, however, is focused on the actual transaction of acquiring goods and services. It is more operational and transactional, dealing with ordering, receiving, and payment processes.

Strategic vs. Tactical

Procurement is a **strategic** function that aligns purchasing decisions with organizational goals. It involves thinking ahead, evaluating long-term needs, and considering how purchasing decisions can affect the overall business performance.

Purchasing is a **tactical** function, concerned with ensuring that specific goods and services are bought in accordance with established requirements. It tends to focus on short-term goals, such as maintaining stock levels or fulfilling immediate operational needs.

Supplier Relationships

Procurement involves **building and managing relationships with suppliers** over time. Procurement professionals work to create partnerships, negotiate favorable terms, and ensure that suppliers meet performance standards. The aim is to establish a reliable supply chain that benefits both parties.

Purchasing, on the other hand, is typically transactional in nature, where the relationship with suppliers is less about partnership and more about fulfilling an immediate need. Purchasing professionals may not have extensive engagement with suppliers beyond ensuring product availability and order fulfillment.

Decision-Making and Planning

Procurement involves **proactive decision-making and planning**. It includes evaluating suppliers, conducting market research, determining the best sourcing strategies, and considering factors such as long-term cost savings, quality, and supplier performance. Procurement professionals are focused on value creation through sourcing decisions.

Purchasing typically involves **reactive decision-making**, where the primary goal is to satisfy the organization's immediate needs. Decisions are made based on pre-determined criteria, such as the lowest price or the quickest delivery time.

Contract and Risk Management

Procurement plays a crucial role in **contract negotiation and management**. Procurement professionals ensure that suppliers meet their obligations and work to manage risks related to price fluctuations, supply chain disruptions, and regulatory compliance. They are also responsible for negotiating terms that benefit the organization in the long run.

Purchasing usually involves fulfilling the terms of contracts that have already been established by the procurement team. Purchasing professionals ensure that orders are placed in accordance with the terms and conditions set forth, but they are not typically involved in the strategic negotiation of contracts or in managing the risks associated with supplier relationships.

Value Creation

Procurement seeks to **optimize value** by considering various factors such as quality, cost, delivery schedules, and supplier capabilities. The procurement process is designed to add value to the organization by selecting suppliers that align with the company's long-term goals and priorities.

Purchasing, by contrast, focuses more on ensuring the **timely and cost-effective acquisition** of goods and services. While cost reduction is important, purchasing does not typically seek to optimize value across the supply chain or work toward long-term improvements.

Overlap Between Procurement and Purchasing

While procurement and purchasing are distinct functions, they are deeply interrelated and often work in tandem. Procurement professionals rely on purchasing to ensure the timely and accurate acquisition of goods, and purchasing professionals depend on procurement strategies to identify the right suppliers and define purchasing requirements.

In practice, the line between procurement and purchasing is not always clear, especially in smaller organizations where both functions may be handled by the same team. For example, a procurement manager may handle both the strategic procurement of goods and services and the tactical tasks of purchasing. However, as organizations grow and their supply chains become more complex, procurement and purchasing functions are often separated, with specialized professionals managing each aspect.

In summary, **procurement** and **purchasing** are both essential aspects of the supply chain and play critical roles in ensuring that an organization has the right goods and services at the right time. Procurement is a **strategic** function focused on adding value, managing risks, and optimizing supplier relationships, while purchasing is a **tactical** function focused on the efficient transaction of buying goods and services. By understanding the distinction between procurement and purchasing, businesses can ensure that both functions work together to support operational efficiency, cost management, and long-term organizational goals.

Chapter 3: Supply Chain Models and Frameworks SCOR

SCOR (Supply Chain Operations Reference) Model

The **SCOR (Supply Chain Operations Reference) Model** is a widely recognized and standardized framework used to assess, improve, and optimize supply chain operations. Developed by the **Supply Chain Council (SCC)**, the SCOR model serves as a valuable tool for businesses seeking to streamline their supply chain processes and improve performance across various supply chain functions. By breaking down the supply chain into specific processes, the SCOR model provides organizations with a structured approach to analyze, measure, and enhance their supply chain activities.

The SCOR model is designed to be adaptable to a variety of industries, organizations, and supply chain types. Its flexibility makes it applicable to companies of all sizes, whether they are involved in manufacturing, retail, or service sectors. Through the SCOR model, companies can align their supply chain processes with best practices, identify performance gaps, and develop strategies for improvement.

Components of the SCOR Model

The SCOR model is built on five core components that serve as the foundation for supply chain management and performance evaluation. These components are designed to help organizations analyze their processes, measure their performance, and implement improvements in a systematic manner.

Plan

The **Plan** process focuses on developing supply chain strategies, forecasting demand, and ensuring that the necessary resources are in place to meet customer requirements. This process involves setting objectives, creating plans, and coordinating activities across the entire supply chain.

Key activities within the **Plan** component include:

Demand planning and forecasting.

Supply chain planning, including capacity and inventory management.

Developing business strategies that align with broader organizational goals.

Resource optimization and balancing supply and demand.

Source

The **Source** process encompasses the activities associated with sourcing materials, components, and services required for production. This phase is critical for establishing and maintaining relationships with suppliers, ensuring that the necessary inputs are available at the right time and place.

Key activities within the **Source** component include:

Supplier selection and qualification.

Purchasing materials, components, and services.

Managing supplier relationships and performance.

Ensuring quality control and compliance with specifications.

Make

The **Make** process refers to the activities involved in transforming raw materials or components into finished goods.

This phase typically focuses on production and manufacturing processes, including scheduling, assembly, and quality control. It also includes activities such as the maintenance of equipment and managing production resources.

Key activities within the **Make** component include:

Manufacturing, assembly, and production scheduling.

Quality control and assurance.

Equipment maintenance and resource management.

Production process improvement and efficiency.

Deliver

The **Deliver** process involves all activities associated with delivering finished goods to customers. This includes managing logistics, warehousing, transportation, and order fulfillment. The goal of this phase is to ensure that products are delivered on time, in full, and in good condition.

Key activities within the **Deliver** component include:

Order management, including order entry, processing, and fulfillment.

Distribution and transportation management.

Warehouse management and inventory control.

Customer relationship management and customer service.

Return

The **Return** process is concerned with handling returns from customers and managing the reverse flow of products. This can involve returns due to defects, damaged goods, or excess inventory. The **Return** process also includes activities related to recycling, refurbishment, and disposal of products.

Key activities within the **Return** component include:

- Managing returns logistics and reverse supply chain operations.

- Handling defective or excess products.

- Refurbishing or recycling products when applicable.

- Analyzing return data to identify root causes and improve product quality.

SCOR Performance Metrics

To assess the effectiveness of supply chain operations, the SCOR model employs a set of **performance metrics** that help organizations measure how well they are performing in each of the five core components. These metrics allow businesses to track progress, identify bottlenecks, and benchmark their performance against industry standards.

The SCOR model defines performance metrics across **three levels**:

Level 1 Metrics (Strategic): These are the high-level, overarching metrics that provide an overview of supply chain performance. The key focus is on customer satisfaction, cost efficiency, and asset management. Some examples of Level 1 metrics include:

Cost: Total supply chain cost, including production, transportation, and storage costs.

Asset Management Efficiency: How efficiently assets are being utilized throughout the supply chain.

Delivery Reliability: The percentage of orders delivered on time and in full.

Customer Satisfaction: Customer feedback, including on-time delivery and product quality.

Level 2 Metrics (Tactical): These metrics provide more detailed insights into specific supply chain functions, such as procurement, production, or logistics. Examples of Level 2 metrics include:

Order Fulfillment Cycle Time: The time it takes from receiving an order to delivering the product to the customer.

Inventory Days of Supply: The number of days inventory is held before it is sold or used in production.

Supplier Performance: Metrics related to the quality, lead times, and reliability of suppliers.

Level 3 Metrics (Operational): These metrics are more granular and focused on the day-to-day operations of the supply chain. Level 3 metrics allow supply chain managers to monitor specific processes, such as inventory turnover or order processing times, and take corrective actions where necessary.

Benefits of the SCOR Model

The SCOR model offers several key benefits to organizations looking to optimize their supply chains and improve operational efficiency:

Standardized Framework: The SCOR model provides a common language and standardized approach to managing and assessing supply chain performance. This allows businesses to benchmark their operations against industry best practices and adopt a more systematic, data-driven approach to improvement.

Process Optimization: By breaking down the supply chain into discrete processes, the SCOR model helps businesses identify inefficiencies and areas for improvement. Organizations can analyze each step in the supply chain and streamline operations to reduce costs, improve cycle times, and enhance customer satisfaction.

Enhanced Visibility and Control: The SCOR model provides organizations with a clearer view of their supply chain operations. By using performance metrics and process mapping, businesses can identify bottlenecks, monitor performance, and gain insights into supplier performance and resource utilization.

Improved Collaboration: SCOR promotes collaboration among supply chain partners, such as suppliers, manufacturers, and distributors. By using standardized processes and performance metrics, organizations can improve coordination and communication, which ultimately leads to a more efficient and responsive supply chain.

Adaptability to Industry Changes: The SCOR model is highly adaptable and can be customized to fit the unique needs of various industries, from manufacturing to services. Its flexibility allows businesses to adjust their supply chain processes in response to changes in market conditions, customer demands, or technological advancements.

Implementing the SCOR Model

Implementing the SCOR model within an organization requires careful planning and alignment with existing processes. The implementation process typically involves the following steps:

Assessment: Conduct a thorough assessment of current supply chain operations to identify gaps and inefficiencies.

Customization: Tailor the SCOR model to meet the specific needs of the organization and industry. This includes selecting appropriate performance metrics and defining processes in alignment with business goals.

Training: Provide training for key stakeholders involved in supply chain operations to ensure that they understand the SCOR model and its applications.

Performance Monitoring: Regularly monitor and evaluate supply chain performance using the SCOR performance metrics. Use the data to make informed decisions and continuously improve operations.

Continuous Improvement: The SCOR model is not a one-time implementation; it requires ongoing monitoring and refinement to ensure that supply chain processes remain efficient and aligned with organizational goals.

The **SCOR (Supply Chain Operations Reference) model** is a powerful framework that offers organizations a structured approach to analyzing, measuring, and improving their supply chain operations. By focusing on key components such as planning, sourcing, making, delivering, and returning, the SCOR model helps businesses optimize processes, reduce costs, improve customer satisfaction, and drive long-term value. With its standardized framework and emphasis on performance metrics, the SCOR model has become an essential tool for organizations seeking to build more efficient, agile, and resilient supply chains in an increasingly complex global marketplace.

Lean and Agile Supply Chain Concepts

In today's competitive and fast-paced business environment, supply chains must be highly efficient, flexible, and responsive to changing market demands. Two critical strategies for achieving these objectives are **lean supply chains** and **agile supply chains**. Both concepts aim to optimize the supply chain, but they differ in their approach, objectives, and execution. Understanding the principles of **lean** and **agile** supply chains, as well as how they can be integrated, is essential for organizations aiming to improve their operational performance and customer satisfaction.

Lean Supply Chain Concept

A **lean supply chain** focuses on minimizing waste and maximizing value. The core idea of lean supply chains is derived from **Lean Manufacturing** principles, which were pioneered by **Toyota** in the 1950s. Lean thinking seeks to eliminate anything that does not add value to the end customer. In the context of supply chain management, lean principles are applied to reduce inefficiencies across all stages of the supply chain, from procurement to delivery.

Key Principles of Lean Supply Chain

> **Elimination of Waste (Muda):** Lean aims to remove all forms of waste (or **muda** in Japanese) in the supply chain. Waste can

take many forms, including overproduction, waiting time, excessive transportation, unnecessary inventory, defective products, and unnecessary processing. By identifying and eliminating waste, companies can improve efficiency and reduce costs.

Just-In-Time (JIT): One of the core concepts of lean supply chains is **Just-In-Time (JIT)**. JIT focuses on producing and delivering products only when they are needed, in the quantity required, and at the right place. This approach helps reduce inventory holding costs and improves cash flow while ensuring that customer demand is met without excess stock.

Continuous Improvement (Kaizen): Lean supply chains emphasize **continuous improvement**, a philosophy known as **kaizen**. This principle encourages organizations to constantly seek opportunities to improve processes, eliminate inefficiencies, and refine workflows. The goal is to create a culture of improvement where everyone in the organization is involved in enhancing supply chain performance.

Standardization of Processes: Lean involves establishing standardized operating procedures to reduce variability and ensure consistency in operations. This standardization helps streamline processes, reduce errors, and improve predictability within the supply chain.

Flow and Pull Systems: Lean supply chains focus on optimizing the flow of materials, information, and products through the system. **Pull systems** are employed, where each step in the production process only pulls materials when they are needed, based on actual demand. This reduces overproduction and minimizes inventory levels.

Benefits of Lean Supply Chain

> **Reduced Costs:** By eliminating waste and improving efficiency, lean supply chains help reduce operational costs, particularly in areas like inventory management, transportation, and production.
>
> **Improved Efficiency:** Lean processes streamline operations, making the entire supply chain more efficient, which leads to faster production times and quicker response to customer demands.
>
> **Better Quality:** Continuous improvement and standardized processes contribute to higher product quality and fewer defects in production.
>
> **Increased Flexibility:** Lean systems that focus on reducing waste also make it easier to scale production or adjust supply chain activities in response to changing demand.

However, while lean is effective in reducing waste and improving efficiency, it may not be sufficient in situations that demand high flexibility or rapid response to market fluctuations. This is where the **agile supply chain** concept comes into play.

Agile Supply Chain Concept

> An **agile supply chain** focuses on flexibility, responsiveness, and the ability to quickly adapt to changing customer demands or market conditions. Unlike lean supply chains, which emphasize cost reduction and efficiency, agile supply chains prioritize the ability to react quickly to uncertainty and variability. Agile supply chains are particularly beneficial in industries where demand is unpredictable, and speed is crucial for customer satisfaction.

Key Principles of Agile Supply Chain

Responsiveness to Demand Fluctuations: The primary goal of an agile supply chain is to be highly responsive to changes in customer demand. By having flexible processes, inventory management practices, and supplier relationships, organizations can quickly adjust their supply chain activities to meet shifting demand patterns.

Postponement: In an agile supply chain, **postponement** refers to delaying the final production or customization of a product until customer demand is clear. This allows companies to hold off on costly investments in finished goods and better match production to actual customer needs.

Collaborative Relationships: Agile supply chains often rely on close collaboration and communication with suppliers, distributors, and customers. By fostering these strong relationships, organizations can gain better visibility into demand and share information more effectively, which helps improve responsiveness.

Inventory Buffering: Unlike lean supply chains that aim to minimize inventory, agile supply chains may hold buffer stocks or **safety stock** to ensure that there is always enough product available to meet unexpected demand surges. This ensures that the supply chain can continue functioning smoothly, even in the face of demand fluctuations or supply disruptions.

Flexibility in Production and Logistics: Agile supply chains incorporate flexible production and logistics systems that can quickly switch between different products or delivery schedules based on changing needs. This flexibility may include the use of modular production systems, flexible manufacturing lines, or multi-skilled workers who can perform different tasks as required.

Benefits of Agile Supply Chain

Improved Responsiveness: Agile supply chains enable companies to respond quickly to changes in demand, market conditions, or customer preferences. This flexibility is essential in industries with high demand volatility, such as fashion, technology, and electronics.

Better Customer Satisfaction: The ability to adapt to customer needs in real-time enhances customer satisfaction and loyalty, as companies can provide faster, more personalized service.

Risk Mitigation: Agile supply chains are better equipped to handle disruptions, such as natural disasters, political instability, or supplier failures. By maintaining flexibility and close supplier relationships, organizations can quickly adjust to mitigate risks and minimize disruptions.

Innovation and Customization: Agile supply chains can more easily accommodate product innovations, customizations, and special customer requests, as they can adjust production and delivery processes to meet specific needs.

However, while agile supply chains are well-suited to environments with high uncertainty, they can sometimes lead to higher costs due to increased inventory levels, expedited transportation, and flexibility in production. In some cases, the ability to maintain agility may require significant investments in technology, processes, and talent.

Lean vs. Agile: Key Differences

While lean and agile supply chains are both aimed at improving supply chain performance, they differ significantly in their priorities and applications.

Focus: Lean supply chains focus on efficiency and waste reduction, whereas agile supply chains prioritize flexibility and responsiveness.

Cost vs. Flexibility: Lean is more cost-oriented and aims to reduce costs through the elimination of waste. Agile, on the other hand, is more focused on maintaining the ability to respond to changing market conditions, which may come at a higher cost.

Inventory Management: Lean supply chains typically aim to minimize inventory levels, while agile supply chains may maintain buffer stock to ensure rapid response to fluctuations in demand.

Risk Mitigation: Lean supply chains reduce risk by optimizing processes and maintaining stable operations. Agile supply chains mitigate risk by ensuring that they can quickly adapt to unexpected disruptions or demand shifts.

Integrating Lean and Agile Supply Chains

In some industries, a hybrid approach that combines the strengths of both lean and agile methodologies—often referred to as the **leagile** supply chain—can provide a powerful solution. By implementing lean principles in stable parts of the supply chain, such as routine production processes, and agile principles in more uncertain areas, such as demand forecasting or new product development, organizations can enjoy the benefits of both approaches.

For example, a company might apply lean principles to manufacturing and production processes where demand is relatively stable and predictable. However, in areas where demand is more volatile, such as fashion or high-tech products, the company could use agile practices to respond to customer needs quickly. By doing so, businesses can achieve both cost-efficiency and flexibility, thereby maximizing value for customers and shareholders.

In conclusion, **lean** and **agile supply chains** represent two critical strategies for optimizing supply chain operations, each offering unique advantages. While **lean** focuses on reducing waste and maximizing efficiency, **agile** emphasizes responsiveness and flexibility to cope with market uncertainties and demand fluctuations. Businesses must carefully evaluate their supply chain environments and customer requirements to determine whether lean, agile, or a combination of both approaches is best suited to their needs. By adopting the right strategy, organizations can enhance their operational performance, mitigate risks, and provide superior value to their customers.

The Bullwhip Effect and its implications

The **bullwhip effect** is a phenomenon in supply chain management that occurs when small fluctuations in customer demand at the retail level escalate into larger and more unpredictable variations in demand at the wholesale, distributor, manufacturer, and supplier levels. Named for its resemblance to the motion of a cracking whip, the effect demonstrates how minor changes in demand can amplify as they move upstream through the supply chain.

This phenomenon is a critical challenge in supply chain management, as it often leads to inefficiencies such as excessive inventory, underutilized production capacity, increased costs, and poor customer service. Understanding the causes, implications, and mitigation strategies for the bullwhip effect is essential for supply chain professionals aiming to maintain stability and optimize operations.

Understanding the Bullwhip Effect

At its core, the bullwhip effect is driven by the way demand information is shared and interpreted across the supply chain. Each participant in the supply chain makes decisions based on their perception of demand, often adding buffers to account for uncertainties. These buffers, combined with delays in communication and order fulfillment, create a ripple effect, amplifying demand variability as it moves upstream.

For example, a slight increase in demand at the retail level may lead retailers to order more from distributors to avoid stockouts. Distributors, interpreting this increase as a sustained trend, may place even larger orders with manufacturers. Manufacturers, in turn, ramp up production and order more raw materials from suppliers, amplifying the original demand fluctuation disproportionately.

Key Causes of the Bullwhip Effect

> **Demand Forecasting Errors:** One of the primary drivers of the bullwhip effect is inaccurate demand forecasting. When supply chain participants rely on historical demand data to predict future needs, even minor forecasting errors can lead to significant overproduction or underproduction.
>
> **Order Batching:** Many organizations place orders in batches to take advantage of economies of scale or reduce administrative costs. However, infrequent, large orders can lead to erratic demand patterns upstream.
>
> **Price Fluctuations and Promotions:** Discounts, promotions, and bulk pricing can distort demand patterns, causing customers to purchase in larger quantities than usual. This artificial spike in demand is often misinterpreted as a long-term trend by upstream participants.
>
> **Inventory Policies and Safety Stocks:** To mitigate the risk of stockouts, supply chain participants often maintain safety stocks. However, these buffer stocks can exacerbate demand variability when multiple tiers in the supply chain add their own safety margins.
>
> **Lack of Information Sharing:** Poor communication and limited visibility across the supply chain mean that participants rely on their own local data rather than a shared understanding of actual end-customer demand.

Lead Time Delays: Longer lead times between order placement and fulfillment amplify the bullwhip effect. Delays create a lag in response to actual demand, causing supply chain participants to overreact to perceived shortages or surpluses.

Implications of the Bullwhip Effect

The bullwhip effect has far-reaching consequences for supply chain performance, affecting costs, efficiency, and customer satisfaction. These implications include:

Operational Inefficiencies

The exaggerated variability in demand leads to frequent adjustments in production schedules, transportation plans, and workforce allocation. These adjustments increase operational complexity and reduce efficiency.

Increased Inventory Costs

To buffer against perceived demand fluctuations, supply chain participants often maintain higher inventory levels. Excessive inventory ties up capital, increases storage costs, and raises the risk of obsolescence for perishable or time-sensitive goods.

Underutilized Capacity

Sudden spikes in orders can strain production capacity, requiring manufacturers to operate at higher costs or invest in additional resources. Conversely, demand slumps can leave capacity underutilized, leading to inefficiencies and lost revenue.

Poor Customer Service

Erratic inventory levels caused by the bullwhip effect can result in stockouts during periods of high demand or excessive stock during demand lulls. Both scenarios lead to dissatisfied customers and potential loss of business.

Higher Supply Chain Costs

The bullwhip effect increases costs across the supply chain, including production, inventory holding, transportation, and order processing costs. These costs ultimately erode profitability and competitiveness.

Strained Supplier Relationships

The variability in order quantities can strain relationships with suppliers, as they struggle to meet fluctuating demands. This can lead to longer lead times, higher prices, or disruptions in supply.

Mitigating the Bullwhip Effect

While the bullwhip effect is a common challenge in supply chain management, it can be mitigated through a combination of process improvements, technology adoption, and collaboration among supply chain participants. Key strategies include:

Improved Demand Forecasting

Using advanced analytics, machine learning, and real-time data, organizations can improve the accuracy of demand forecasts. Forecasting tools that integrate data from multiple sources, such as point-of-sale (POS) systems, market trends, and historical patterns, can provide a clearer picture of actual demand.

Collaborative Planning and Information Sharing

Collaboration among supply chain partners, such as through **Collaborative Planning, Forecasting, and Replenishment (CPFR)**, helps align demand and supply planning. Sharing real-time data, including sales forecasts and inventory levels, reduces uncertainty and prevents overreaction to demand changes.

Reduction of Lead Times

Shortening lead times through streamlined production processes, faster transportation methods, or local sourcing reduces the lag between order placement and fulfillment. This minimizes the risk of overreaction to demand fluctuations.

Adoption of Just-In-Time (JIT) Practices

JIT practices aim to align production and inventory levels closely with actual demand. While JIT reduces waste and excess inventory, it requires robust communication and coordination among supply chain partners.

Stabilization of Pricing Policies

Avoiding frequent price changes, promotions, or bulk discounts prevents artificial spikes in demand. Stable pricing encourages steady buying patterns and reduces variability in order quantities.

Implementation of Technology

Technologies such as **Enterprise Resource Planning (ERP)** systems, **Supply Chain Management (SCM)** software, and **Internet of Things (IoT)** devices improve visibility and coordination across the supply chain. These tools enable real-time tracking, data sharing, and demand synchronization.

Smaller Order Batches

Encouraging more frequent, smaller orders instead of large, infrequent ones reduces variability. Digital platforms and automated ordering systems can help manage the administrative costs of smaller order sizes.

The bullwhip effect remains a significant challenge in supply chain management, but it also offers an opportunity for improvement. By understanding the root causes and implications of this phenomenon, organizations can implement strategies to minimize its impact. From enhancing demand forecasting and fostering collaboration to leveraging technology and stabilizing pricing, there are multiple pathways to mitigating the bullwhip effect. For professionals in supply chain management, addressing this issue not only improves operational efficiency but also strengthens customer relationships, reduces costs, and enhances the overall competitiveness of the supply chain. In an increasingly dynamic global marketplace, controlling the bullwhip effect is a critical step toward building resilient and responsive supply chains.

Part 2: Strategic Procurement Chapter

4: Procurement Planning

Developing procurement strategies aligned with business objectives.

Effective procurement planning is a cornerstone of strategic procurement, playing a pivotal role in aligning organizational purchasing efforts with overarching business objectives. It ensures that procurement activities contribute to achieving competitive advantage, operational efficiency, and long-term sustainability. In today's rapidly evolving business landscape, organizations must craft procurement strategies that not only address immediate needs but also anticipate future challenges and opportunities.

The Role of Procurement in Business Strategy

Procurement is no longer a back-office function confined to transactional purchasing; it has evolved into a strategic discipline integral to achieving business goals. Whether the aim is cost reduction, risk mitigation, innovation, or sustainability, procurement provides the framework for managing external spend and supplier relationships effectively.

Procurement strategies must align with the organization's vision, mission, and values. For instance, a company focusing on innovation may prioritize sourcing cutting-edge materials or technologies, while an organization committed to sustainability may emphasize eco-friendly suppliers and ethical sourcing practices. In this context, procurement becomes a key enabler of strategic objectives, translating high-level goals into actionable plans.

Key Principles of Procurement Strategy Development

Developing procurement strategies that align with business objectives requires a structured approach based on several guiding principles:

Business Alignment: Procurement strategies must reflect the organization's broader strategic priorities, including financial targets, market positioning, and growth objectives.

Value Creation: The focus should extend beyond cost savings to include innovation, quality, and long-term value creation.

Risk Management: Proactively identifying and mitigating risks in the supply chain ensures continuity and resilience.

Sustainability and Ethics: Modern procurement strategies increasingly incorporate environmental, social, and governance (ESG) considerations.

Agility and Flexibility: Strategies must be adaptable to changing market dynamics, technological advancements, and evolving business needs.

Steps in Developing Procurement Strategies

Understanding Business Objectives The first step in developing a procurement strategy is gaining a deep understanding of the organization's strategic goals. This requires close collaboration with key stakeholders, including senior management, operations, marketing, and finance teams. For example, if a company aims to expand into new markets, procurement must identify suppliers who can support the required scalability and regional compliance.

Analyzing Spend and Supply Market Comprehensive spend analysis provides insights into where money is being spent, with whom, and on what terms. This data forms the foundation for identifying opportunities to optimize costs, consolidate suppliers, or leverage economies of scale. Simultaneously, market analysis helps assess supplier capabilities, competitive landscapes, and emerging trends, enabling informed decision-making.

Segmenting Procurement Categories Segmentation involves categorizing procurement activities based on their strategic importance and complexity. Tools such as the **Kraljic Matrix** classify items into categories like strategic, leverage, bottleneck, and non-critical, guiding resource allocation and supplier management efforts. For instance, strategic items warrant long-term partnerships, while non-critical items may be sourced through transactional relationships.

Defining Strategic Priorities Procurement strategies must prioritize areas that deliver the greatest impact on business objectives. For example, a manufacturing company might focus on securing reliable raw material supplies to ensure production continuity, while a technology firm might prioritize vendor partnerships that drive innovation.

Setting Performance Metrics Key Performance Indicators (KPIs) provide a measurable framework for evaluating the success of procurement strategies. Metrics such as cost savings, supplier performance, and contract compliance align procurement efforts with business outcomes. Moreover, KPIs should be reviewed periodically to ensure relevance and alignment with evolving goals.

Developing Supplier Relationships Building strong relationships with suppliers is critical to achieving strategic objectives. Collaborative supplier relationships foster innovation, enhance quality, and ensure timely delivery. Techniques such as Supplier Relationship Management (SRM) and supplier scorecards facilitate ongoing engagement and performance monitoring.

Incorporating Technology and Innovation Digital tools and platforms are transforming procurement strategies. Technologies like **e-procurement systems, blockchain for supply chain transparency, and AI-driven analytics** enhance decision-making, streamline processes, and provide real-time insights. Leveraging these technologies enables procurement teams to focus on strategic activities rather than transactional tasks.

Integrating Risk Management A robust procurement strategy includes mechanisms for identifying and mitigating risks such as supplier insolvency, geopolitical instability, or supply chain disruptions. Diversifying the supplier base, incorporating contingency plans, and monitoring geopolitical trends are essential components of a risk-aware strategy.

Procurement as a Driver of Competitive Advantage

Strategic procurement provides organizations with a competitive edge by optimizing costs, enhancing supplier relationships, and fostering innovation. By aligning procurement activities with business objectives, companies can unlock opportunities for growth, efficiency, and differentiation. For instance, leveraging strategic sourcing can improve product quality while reducing time-to-market, ultimately enhancing customer satisfaction and brand reputation.

Case Study: Aligning Procurement with Business Goals

Consider a global retail company aiming to expand its presence in emerging markets. The organization's business objective is to establish a supply chain capable of supporting rapid growth while maintaining cost efficiency. To align procurement with this objective, the company implemented the following strategies:

- Conducted a detailed spend analysis to identify cost-saving opportunities and potential supplier consolidations.

- Partnered with regional suppliers to reduce lead times and improve responsiveness to market demands.

- Adopted a digital procurement platform to enhance transparency, streamline processes, and enable real-time decision-making.

- Established sustainability targets, prioritizing suppliers with robust ESG credentials to align with the company's corporate social responsibility goals.

As a result, the company not only achieved its expansion goals but also improved its overall supply chain efficiency and brand reputation.

Challenges in Procurement Strategy Development

Despite its benefits, developing procurement strategies aligned with business objectives is not without challenges. Common obstacles include:

- **Stakeholder Misalignment:** Divergent priorities among stakeholders can hinder the alignment process.

- **Data Limitations:** Incomplete or inaccurate data can compromise spend analysis and forecasting efforts.

- **Supplier Resistance:** Suppliers may resist changes in terms or practices that conflict with their interests.

- **Market Volatility:** Fluctuating market conditions, such as raw material price increases or geopolitical tensions, can disrupt procurement plans.

Addressing these challenges requires a combination of clear communication, robust data analytics, and adaptive planning.

Conclusion

Procurement planning is an essential strategic function that connects organizational goals with the external supply landscape. By developing procurement strategies aligned with business objectives, companies can drive operational excellence, foster innovation, and build resilient supply chains. For procurement professionals, this alignment is both an opportunity and a responsibility, requiring a proactive approach, strategic thinking, and a commitment to continuous improvement. As businesses navigate an increasingly dynamic global environment, strategic procurement planning will remain a critical enabler of success.

Category Management and Spend Analysis

In the realm of modern procurement, category management and spend analysis are indispensable strategies that enable organizations to optimize their procurement processes, enhance supplier relationships, and drive cost efficiency. These tools go beyond transactional procurement by introducing a structured, strategic approach to managing spend categories and uncovering insights that lead to informed decision-making.

Understanding Category Management

Category management is a strategic approach to organizing procurement activities around specific categories of goods or services. Instead of treating procurement as a series of individual purchases, category management groups related items into categories and develops tailored strategies to manage each one. This approach ensures alignment with business objectives, better control over spending, and stronger supplier relationships.

For instance, a manufacturing company may have categories such as raw materials, maintenance, repair and operations (MRO), and logistics services. By managing each category strategically, the company can address the unique challenges and opportunities within each domain, such as securing bulk discounts for raw materials or identifying cost-effective transportation providers.

The Role of Category Managers

A critical aspect of category management is the role of the category manager. These professionals act as subject matter experts for their assigned categories, analyzing market trends, identifying cost-saving opportunities, and fostering supplier collaboration. They work cross-functionally with stakeholders from finance, operations, and supply chain to ensure category strategies align with organizational goals.

Category managers also engage in supplier negotiations, develop long-term sourcing plans, and monitor supplier performance through key metrics. Their expertise ensures that procurement decisions within each category contribute to the broader success of the business.

Benefits of Category Management

Category management offers numerous advantages, including:

Enhanced Cost Efficiency: Grouping purchases by category allows for bulk procurement, leveraging economies of scale, and negotiating better contract terms.

Improved Supplier Relationships: By developing tailored strategies for each category, organizations can foster deeper, more collaborative partnerships with key suppliers.

Risk Mitigation: Category-specific risk assessments enable organizations to anticipate and mitigate supply chain disruptions.

Alignment with Business Goals: Strategic category management ensures procurement efforts align with the organization's overall objectives, such as sustainability or innovation.

Market Insights: Focused category analysis helps organizations stay ahead of market trends, such as price fluctuations or emerging technologies.

Implementing Category Management

The implementation of category management involves several key steps:

Spend Analysis Understanding the organization's spending patterns is the foundation of effective category management. This involves analyzing historical data to identify where money is being spent, on what goods or services, and with which suppliers. For example, an organization may discover that it is purchasing similar items from multiple suppliers, leading to inefficiencies and missed opportunities for volume discounts.

Category Definition Once spending patterns are understood, procurement teams define categories based on logical groupings of goods or services. Categories may be broad, such as IT equipment, or narrowly focused, such as cloud computing services. Clear definitions ensure that all related spending is captured and managed under the appropriate category.

Strategy Development For each category, procurement teams develop strategies that address specific objectives. For instance, the strategy for IT equipment might focus on securing cost-effective suppliers for standardized products, while the strategy for cloud services might prioritize performance and scalability.

Supplier Engagement Engaging with suppliers within each category is essential for executing category strategies. This involves conducting market research, issuing requests for proposals (RFPs), and negotiating contracts that align with the organization's goals.

Performance Monitoring Ongoing monitoring of category performance ensures that strategies remain effective and relevant. Key Performance Indicators (KPIs), such as cost savings, supplier reliability, and delivery timelines, provide measurable benchmarks for success.

Understanding Spend Analysis

Spend analysis is a complementary tool to category management, focusing on the systematic examination of organizational expenditures to uncover insights and opportunities. It involves collecting, categorizing, and analyzing procurement data to gain a comprehensive understanding of spending patterns.

The Objectives of Spend Analysis

The primary objectives of spend analysis include:

Identifying Savings Opportunities: By analyzing spending data, organizations can identify areas where costs can be reduced, such as consolidating suppliers or renegotiating contracts.

Improving Procurement Processes: Spend analysis highlights inefficiencies in procurement practices, enabling organizations to streamline processes and reduce administrative overhead.

Enhancing Supplier Performance: Understanding spending patterns with specific suppliers allows organizations to assess their performance and explore opportunities for improved collaboration.

Mitigating Risks: By identifying reliance on single suppliers or regions, spend analysis helps organizations anticipate and mitigate potential risks in the supply chain.

Supporting Strategic Decision-Making: Spend analysis provides the data-driven insights necessary for informed procurement decisions and strategy development.

Key Steps in Spend Analysis

Data Collection The first step in spend analysis is collecting procurement data from various sources, such as purchase orders, invoices, and supplier contracts. This data must be accurate, complete, and up-to-date to ensure meaningful analysis.

Data Categorization Categorizing spending data involves grouping expenditures into logical categories, often aligned with the organization's category management framework. Tools such as procurement software can automate this process, ensuring consistency and accuracy.

Data Analysis Once data is categorized, procurement teams analyze it to uncover patterns and trends. This may involve calculating metrics such as total spend by category, spend by supplier, or spend by region. Advanced analytics tools, such as AI-powered platforms, can identify hidden correlations and opportunities.

Insights and Recommendations The final step is translating analytical findings into actionable insights. For example, spend analysis might reveal that the organization is over-reliant on a single supplier for critical components, prompting diversification efforts.

Integrating Spend Analysis with Category Management

Spend analysis and category management are mutually reinforcing strategies. Spend analysis provides the data-driven insights necessary to define categories, develop strategies, and monitor performance. Conversely, category management ensures that spend analysis efforts are aligned with broader procurement goals and organizational objectives.

For example, a spend analysis might reveal that a company's MRO spending is fragmented across multiple suppliers. In response, the category manager for MRO could develop a strategy to consolidate spending with a select group of suppliers, negotiating better terms and improving operational efficiency.

Case Study: Leveraging Category Management and Spend Analysis

A global pharmaceutical company faced rising procurement costs and supply chain inefficiencies. By implementing category management and spend analysis, the organization achieved significant improvements:

Conducted a comprehensive spend analysis, identifying high-cost categories and fragmented supplier relationships.

Defined strategic categories, such as raw materials, packaging, and logistics, each managed by dedicated category managers.

Developed category-specific strategies, such as consolidating raw material suppliers and optimizing packaging designs for cost efficiency.

Monitored performance using KPIs, achieving a 15% reduction in procurement costs within two years.

Category management and spend analysis are transformative tools for modern procurement. By strategically managing procurement categories and leveraging data-driven insights, organizations can achieve cost efficiency, enhance supplier relationships, and align procurement efforts with business objectives. For professionals in procurement and supply chain management, mastering these strategies is essential for driving organizational success in a competitive global marketplace.

Make-or-Buy Decisions

The make-or-buy decision is one of the most critical and strategic choices an organization faces in its operations. It involves determining whether to produce a product or service in-house (make) or to outsource its production to an external supplier (buy). This decision impacts cost structures, resource allocation, control over processes, quality, and long-term organizational strategy. As businesses strive for competitive advantage in a dynamic market, the make-or-buy decision becomes a pivotal element in shaping their operational and strategic pathways.

Understanding the Make-or-Buy Concept

At its core, the make-or-buy decision evaluates the comparative advantages of internal production versus external procurement. It requires a thorough assessment of an organization's capabilities, costs, and strategic objectives. Making a product in-house can offer greater control over quality and intellectual property, while buying from an external supplier may provide cost savings, flexibility, and access to specialized expertise. This trade-off lies at the heart of the make-or-buy decision-making process.

The complexity of these decisions arises from the multitude of factors that need to be considered. These include direct and indirect costs, capacity constraints, supplier reliability, market trends, and the organization's long-term goals. For example, a company with excess production capacity might lean toward making components in-house, while one facing resource limitations could find outsourcing more attractive.

Strategic Importance of Make-or-Buy Decisions

Make-or-buy decisions are not merely operational choices; they are strategic determinations that align with an organization's broader objectives. These decisions influence core competencies, risk management, and the ability to respond to changing market conditions. For instance, a technology firm may decide to produce its proprietary chips in-house to safeguard intellectual property, even if external suppliers could manufacture them at a lower cost.

Strategic considerations also extend to supply chain dynamics. Outsourcing can introduce risks such as dependency on suppliers, supply chain disruptions, and loss of control over critical processes. Conversely, in-house production might limit an organization's ability to scale rapidly or pivot to new technologies. Balancing these factors is essential for achieving strategic alignment and sustaining competitive advantage.

Key Factors Influencing Make-or-Buy Decisions

Several factors shape the make-or-buy decision, requiring organizations to adopt a holistic and analytical approach.

Cost Considerations
Cost analysis is a foundational element in make-or-buy decisions. Organizations must evaluate the total cost of ownership (TCO) for both in-house production and outsourcing. This includes direct costs such as raw materials, labor, and manufacturing overheads, as well as indirect costs like administrative expenses, logistics, and quality assurance.

Outsourcing may appear cost-effective at first glance due to lower labor costs in certain regions or economies of scale achieved by suppliers. However, hidden costs, such as supplier management, transportation, and potential quality issues, can erode these savings. In contrast, in-house production may require significant upfront investments in infrastructure and technology, which need to be amortized over time.

Core Competencies
An organization's core competencies play a vital role in the make-or-buy decision. Producing goods or services that align with the organization's unique strengths can enhance efficiency, innovation, and differentiation. For example, an automotive manufacturer may choose to produce engines in-house, leveraging its engineering expertise, while outsourcing non-critical components such as upholstery.

Outsourcing activities outside the organization's core competencies allows businesses to focus on their strengths while benefiting from the expertise of specialized suppliers. This strategic outsourcing can drive innovation and agility, enabling the organization to respond swiftly to market changes.

Quality and Control
Quality requirements and control considerations often tip the scale in make-or-buy decisions. In-house production provides greater control over quality standards, processes, and timelines. This is particularly critical for industries with stringent regulatory requirements, such as pharmaceuticals or aerospace.

However, outsourcing does not necessarily equate to compromised quality. By partnering with reputable and certified suppliers, organizations can achieve high-quality outcomes while focusing their internal resources on other priorities. Effective supplier relationship management and robust contract agreements are essential to maintaining quality when outsourcing.

Capacity and Resource Availability
An organization's existing capacity and resource constraints significantly influence make-or-buy decisions. Companies with underutilized facilities may opt for in-house production to maximize the return on existing assets. Conversely, organizations facing resource

shortages, such as skilled labor or advanced technology, might find outsourcing a more viable option.

For instance, a startup in the consumer electronics sector may lack the resources to manufacture its products in-house and instead choose to partner with a contract manufacturer. As the company scales and gains resources, it might revisit the decision to internalize production.

Supply Chain and Market Dynamics
Market conditions and supply chain factors play a pivotal role in make-or-buy decisions. Outsourcing can provide access to suppliers with established networks, enabling faster time-to-market and cost efficiency. However, dependency on external suppliers introduces risks such as price volatility, geopolitical uncertainties, and supply chain disruptions.

Organizations must also consider market trends, such as increasing demand for sustainability and ethical sourcing. Producing in-house allows companies to align with these trends by implementing green practices and maintaining transparency. Alternatively, businesses can partner with suppliers who share their commitment to sustainability.

Risk Management
Risk considerations are central to make-or-buy decisions. Producing in-house mitigates risks associated with supplier dependency, such as delays, quality issues, or confidentiality breaches. However, it introduces other risks, such as production disruptions due to equipment failures or labor shortages.

Outsourcing, on the other hand, diversifies risk by leveraging a supplier's infrastructure and expertise. Effective risk management strategies, such as dual sourcing or maintaining a balance between in-house and outsourced production, can help mitigate potential vulnerabilities.

Case Studies in Make-or-Buy Decisions

Examining real-world examples illustrates the complexities and outcomes of make-or-buy decisions.

A global technology company faced a dilemma regarding the production of its semiconductor chips. Outsourcing to established foundries offered cost savings and faster production timelines, but the company decided to build its own fabrication facility. This decision was driven by the strategic importance of chip design, the need for confidentiality, and the opportunity to innovate without external constraints.

In contrast, a mid-sized apparel manufacturer outsourced its logistics operations to a third-party provider. This decision allowed the company to focus on its core competency—design and production—while benefiting from the logistics provider's expertise in supply chain optimization and global distribution.

Balancing Short-Term and Long-Term Objectives

Make-or-buy decisions often involve balancing short-term cost savings with long-term strategic goals. While outsourcing may provide immediate financial benefits, it can limit an organization's flexibility and control over critical processes. Conversely, in-house production requires significant investment but offers greater potential for innovation and scalability.

Organizations must adopt a dynamic approach to make-or-buy decisions, revisiting them periodically as market conditions, technology, and internal capabilities evolve. A well-considered decision today might require adjustment in the future to align with changing business landscapes.

The make-or-buy decision is a cornerstone of strategic procurement and supply chain management. It requires a comprehensive analysis of costs, competencies, quality, capacity, risks, and market dynamics. By aligning these factors with organizational goals, businesses can make informed decisions that drive efficiency, innovation, and competitive advantage. Whether choosing to make or buy, the key lies in adopting a balanced, flexible approach that positions the organization for long-term success in an ever-changing marketplace.

Chapter 5: Supplier Selection and Evaluation

Criteria for Supplier Selection

Selecting the right suppliers is a cornerstone of effective procurement and supply chain management. The choice of suppliers influences not only the quality and cost of products or services but also an organization's ability to meet customer expectations, manage risks, and achieve strategic objectives. Supplier selection is not merely a transactional activity; it is a strategic process that requires careful consideration of various criteria to ensure alignment with the organization's operational needs and long-term goals.

Understanding the Importance of Supplier Selection

Suppliers play a critical role in an organization's supply chain ecosystem. They provide the raw materials, components, or services that enable the organization to deliver value to its customers. Poor supplier choices can result in disruptions, quality issues, increased costs, and reputational damage. Conversely, selecting the right suppliers fosters collaboration, innovation, and efficiency.

The supplier selection process is both art and science. It combines quantitative methods, such as cost analysis and performance metrics, with qualitative assessments, such as trust and cultural fit. This dual approach ensures a holistic evaluation, helping organizations build strong and reliable partnerships.

Key Criteria for Supplier Selection

When evaluating potential suppliers, organizations typically assess them against a set of predefined criteria. These criteria serve as benchmarks to compare and select the best fit for the organization's needs. While the specific weightage of each criterion may vary based on the industry and business priorities, certain factors are universally significant.

1. Cost and Pricing
Cost remains a primary consideration in supplier selection, as it directly affects the organization's profitability. However, the focus is not solely

on the lowest price. Organizations evaluate the total cost of ownership (TCO), which includes purchase price, shipping costs, tariffs, maintenance, and potential downtime due to quality or delivery issues.

While low-cost suppliers may seem appealing, they can pose risks such as subpar quality or unreliable delivery schedules. A balanced approach involves seeking suppliers that offer competitive pricing without compromising on other critical factors like quality and service.

2. Quality Standards
Quality is a non-negotiable criterion in supplier selection. The quality of inputs directly influences the end product or service, customer satisfaction, and brand reputation. Organizations assess a supplier's adherence to quality standards through certifications, such as ISO 9001, and by reviewing sample products, quality audit reports, and customer feedback.

Suppliers with robust quality control processes demonstrate a commitment to consistency and reliability. They are better equipped to meet the organization's specifications and regulatory requirements, minimizing risks and ensuring a high level of customer satisfaction.

3. Delivery Reliability
Timely delivery is critical for maintaining smooth operations and meeting customer commitments. A supplier's track record in meeting deadlines and fulfilling orders without delays or disruptions is a key selection criterion.

Organizations evaluate suppliers' logistical capabilities, including inventory management, transportation networks, and lead times. Suppliers with advanced forecasting and planning systems are more likely to align with the organization's production schedules and market demands.

4. Financial Stability
The financial health of a supplier is an indicator of their ability to sustain operations and invest in innovation. Financially stable suppliers

are less likely to face disruptions, such as bankruptcy or cash flow shortages, which could affect their ability to deliver on commitments.

Organizations typically review a supplier's financial statements, credit ratings, and history of performance during economic downturns. Long-term partnerships are best forged with suppliers that demonstrate financial resilience and the capacity to grow alongside the organization.

5. Technological Capabilities
In an era of rapid technological advancement, suppliers with cutting-edge capabilities and innovative approaches are valuable partners. Organizations assess a supplier's investment in technology, research and development (R&D), and ability to adopt new processes or systems.

For industries reliant on innovation, such as electronics or pharmaceuticals, suppliers with a forward-thinking mindset contribute to the organization's competitive advantage. Collaborative innovation efforts, such as co-development of new products, often hinge on a supplier's technological expertise.

6. Compliance with Regulatory and Ethical Standards
Compliance with laws, regulations, and ethical standards is a fundamental criterion in supplier selection. Suppliers must adhere to industry-specific regulations, environmental norms, labor laws, and ethical practices.

Organizations evaluate a supplier's compliance through certifications, audits, and policy reviews. Increasingly, businesses prioritize suppliers that align with their sustainability goals, such as reducing carbon footprints or using ethically sourced materials.

7. Flexibility and Scalability
The ability to adapt to changing demands is an essential attribute for suppliers. Organizations seek suppliers that can scale production up or down based on market conditions, seasonal fluctuations, or unexpected disruptions.

Flexibility also includes the capacity to customize products or services to meet specific requirements. Suppliers that demonstrate agility in responding to new demands or challenges are better equipped to support dynamic business environments.

8. Geographic Location

The geographic location of a supplier affects transportation costs, lead times, and potential risks. Proximity to the organization's facilities or end markets can enhance responsiveness and reduce logistical complexities.

However, global sourcing often offers cost advantages and access to specialized skills or materials. Organizations weigh the benefits of local versus global suppliers, considering factors like geopolitical stability, trade policies, and currency exchange risks.

9. Communication and Cultural Fit

Effective communication and alignment in organizational culture are critical for building successful supplier relationships. Suppliers that share the organization's values and approach to problem-solving are more likely to foster trust and collaboration.

Strong communication channels ensure clarity in expectations, faster resolution of issues, and alignment in strategic objectives. Cultural fit, particularly in international partnerships, reduces misunderstandings and enhances the overall working relationship.

10. Reputation and References

The reputation of a supplier serves as an indicator of their reliability, professionalism, and track record. Organizations often seek references from existing customers to validate the supplier's performance. Positive feedback and testimonials reinforce confidence in the supplier's capabilities.

Conversely, a history of disputes, poor customer service, or recurring issues raises red flags. A thorough reputation check, including online reviews and industry networks, provides valuable insights into a supplier's credibility.

Integrating Criteria into the Selection Process

To ensure a structured and objective evaluation, organizations often use scoring systems or supplier selection matrices. These tools assign weightages to each criterion based on its relevance to the organization's goals. Potential suppliers are then scored against these criteria, enabling a data-driven decision-making process.

For example, an organization in the automotive industry might prioritize quality and delivery reliability, while a technology startup might emphasize cost and innovation. The scoring system reflects these priorities, guiding the selection process toward the most suitable supplier.

The criteria for supplier selection form the foundation of a robust procurement strategy. By evaluating suppliers against comprehensive and well-defined benchmarks, organizations can mitigate risks, enhance efficiency, and build strong, collaborative partnerships. In a competitive business environment, the ability to select the right suppliers is not just a procurement function—it is a strategic advantage that drives long-term success.

Vendor Evaluation Tools: RFI, RFQ, and RFP

Selecting the right vendor is a strategic decision that impacts an organization's operational efficiency, cost structure, and overall performance. To make informed and objective choices, procurement professionals rely on systematic tools such as Request for Information (RFI), Request for Quotation (RFQ), and Request for Proposal (RFP). Each tool serves a distinct purpose and is applied at different stages of the vendor evaluation process. Understanding the nuances of these tools is essential for crafting a robust procurement strategy.

The Role of Vendor Evaluation Tools in Procurement

Vendor evaluation tools enable organizations to gather, compare, and analyze information from potential suppliers. These tools structure communication between the buyer and suppliers, ensuring clarity, transparency, and alignment of expectations. The choice of tool depends on the complexity of the procurement need, the nature of the market, and the organization's strategic priorities.

By using RFI, RFQ, and RFP strategically, procurement teams can reduce risks, optimize costs, and foster long-term supplier relationships. These tools also facilitate a competitive process, ensuring that the organization selects the best vendor based on objective criteria.

Request for Information (RFI)

An RFI is an initial step in the vendor evaluation process. It is used when an organization seeks to gather broad information about potential suppliers, products, or services. RFIs are typically employed in the exploratory phase, where the organization is not yet ready to make a purchase decision but aims to understand the market landscape.

Purpose of RFI

The primary purpose of an RFI is to collect qualitative and quantitative data that helps the organization refine its requirements and shortlist potential vendors. It is particularly useful when entering a new market, sourcing a new category, or evaluating emerging technologies. RFIs often focus on the supplier's capabilities, experience, certifications, and alignment with the buyer's objectives.

Content of an RFI

An RFI typically includes questions about the vendor's:

- Company background, including size, financial stability, and market presence

Product or service offerings, highlighting features and differentiators.

  Technological capabilities, such as systems integration or innovation capacity.

  Compliance with industry standards and certifications.

  Geographic coverage and logistical capabilities.

RFIs are not binding and do not involve pricing discussions. Instead, they provide a foundation for moving to the next phase, where more detailed and specific information is gathered.

When to Use RFI
Organizations use RFIs when they:

  Lack familiarity with the supplier market.

  Need to identify qualified vendors for a complex requirement.

  Wish to explore multiple options before narrowing down to a select few.

Request for Quotation (RFQ)

An RFQ is a procurement tool used when the requirements are clear, and the primary objective is to obtain competitive pricing. RFQs focus on cost-related aspects and are suitable for commodities, standardized products, or services with well-defined specifications.

Purpose of RFQ
The RFQ process aims to ensure cost efficiency by inviting suppliers to submit detailed price quotations. It is transactional in nature and emphasizes measurable attributes like unit cost, delivery timelines, and

payment terms. The RFQ stage typically follows an RFI or serves as the initial tool when the requirements are straightforward.

Content of an RFQ
An RFQ includes detailed specifications, such as:

> Product or service descriptions, including quantities, quality standards, and performance requirements.
>
> Delivery schedules and locations.
>
> Payment terms and conditions.
>
> Penalties for non-compliance or delays.

Suppliers respond with itemized quotes, often accompanied by additional terms like bulk discounts or warranty options. Unlike RFIs, RFQs result in binding offers that form the basis for contract negotiation.

When to Use RFQ
RFQs are most effective when:

> The product or service is commoditized or standardized.
>
> The organization seeks the most competitive pricing for a specific need.
>
> Requirements are well-defined, leaving little room for interpretation.

Challenges with RFQs
While RFQs are efficient for cost-focused procurement, they may not address qualitative factors like innovation, collaboration potential, or long-term value. Organizations must ensure that their emphasis on pricing does not compromise other critical attributes.

Request for Proposal (RFP)

An RFP is a comprehensive tool used when the procurement need is complex, and the organization seeks detailed proposals from suppliers. RFPs go beyond cost considerations, evaluating vendors on multiple dimensions such as technical capabilities, solution design, and strategic fit.

Purpose of RFP
The RFP process is designed to facilitate a holistic evaluation of potential suppliers. It helps organizations identify vendors that offer the best overall value, balancing cost, quality, innovation, and long-term benefits. RFPs are typically used for strategic or high-value projects where collaboration and customization are critical.

Content of an RFP
An RFP includes detailed requirements and evaluation criteria, such as:

Project scope and objectives, outlining the organization's needs and expectations.

Technical specifications, detailing functionality, performance, and integration requirements.

Evaluation criteria, highlighting weightages for cost, quality, innovation, and other factors.

Proposal format, specifying sections like technical solution, project plan, and risk mitigation strategies.

Contract terms and conditions, including service-level agreements (SLAs) and key performance indicators (KPIs).

RFPs require suppliers to provide in-depth responses, including technical solutions, implementation plans, resource allocation, and cost breakdowns. This level of detail enables a thorough comparison of vendors' capabilities and proposals.

When to Use RFP
RFPs are ideal for:

High-value or strategic procurement projects.

Situations where multiple evaluation criteria are equally important.

Complex requirements that necessitate tailored solutions or innovation.

Benefits of RFPs
RFPs promote competition and transparency, ensuring that the organization considers a wide range of factors. They also foster collaboration, as suppliers often engage in discussions or clarifications to refine their proposals.

Challenges with RFPs
The RFP process can be time-consuming and resource-intensive for both buyers and suppliers. Crafting a detailed RFP and reviewing complex proposals requires careful planning and expertise. Additionally, the subjective nature of qualitative evaluations may introduce biases, necessitating clear and objective scoring frameworks.

Integrating RFI, RFQ, and RFP in Vendor Evaluation

RFI, RFQ, and RFP are not mutually exclusive; they can be used in combination to ensure a comprehensive evaluation process. For instance, an organization might begin with an RFI to understand the market, follow up with an RFQ for standardized needs, and issue an RFP for a complex project.

By aligning the tools with the procurement strategy, organizations can balance efficiency, cost-effectiveness, and strategic value. Effective use of these tools requires clear communication, well-defined requirements, and a structured evaluation process.

Conclusion

RFI, RFQ, and RFP are indispensable tools in modern procurement. They empower organizations to make informed decisions, minimize risks, and achieve optimal outcomes. By understanding the purpose and application of each tool, procurement professionals can navigate the complexities of vendor evaluation with confidence and precision, ensuring alignment with organizational objectives and market dynamics.

Supplier Performance Management

Supplier performance management (SPM) is a critical aspect of procurement and supply chain strategy. It involves systematically evaluating, monitoring, and improving the performance of suppliers to ensure they meet or exceed the organization's expectations. Effective SPM contributes to operational efficiency, cost savings, risk mitigation, and long-term value creation in supplier relationships. For organizations that rely on a network of suppliers, mastering supplier performance management is essential to maintaining a competitive edge in the market.

The Importance of Supplier Performance Management

Suppliers play a pivotal role in the value chain, directly impacting product quality, service delivery, and customer satisfaction. As businesses face increasing pressure to enhance operational efficiency and deliver value to stakeholders, managing supplier performance becomes a strategic priority.

SPM is important for several reasons:

> **Quality Assurance**: Ensures that suppliers consistently deliver products or services that meet predefined quality standards.

Cost Control: Identifies inefficiencies or cost-saving opportunities within the supplier relationship.

Risk Mitigation: Helps detect and address potential risks, such as delays, non-compliance, or financial instability.

Innovation and Collaboration: Encourages suppliers to innovate and align with the organization's strategic goals.

Sustainability: Monitors adherence to sustainability and ethical standards, aligning with corporate social responsibility (CSR) objectives.

Without a robust supplier performance management framework, organizations risk supply disruptions, increased costs, and reputational damage.

Key Components of Supplier Performance Management

A successful SPM system integrates various components that collectively ensure supplier effectiveness and alignment with organizational objectives. These components include:

Defining Key Performance Indicators (KPIs)

SPM begins with the identification of measurable KPIs tailored to the organization's goals and industry standards. Common KPIs include:

On-Time Delivery (OTD): Measures the supplier's ability to meet agreed delivery schedules.

Defect Rate: Tracks the frequency and severity of defects or non-conformance in products or services.

Cost Variance: Assesses deviations from agreed-upon costs or budgets.

Responsiveness: Evaluates the supplier's agility in addressing issues or fulfilling urgent requirements.

Sustainability Metrics: Monitors compliance with environmental and ethical standards.

Well-defined KPIs provide a clear basis for evaluating supplier performance objectively and consistently.

Performance Monitoring and Data Collection

Effective SPM relies on continuous monitoring and the collection of performance data. This process involves using various tools and systems, such as enterprise resource planning (ERP) software, supplier scorecards, and real-time dashboards. Accurate and up-to-date data ensures that the organization has a comprehensive view of supplier performance across multiple dimensions.

Supplier Audits and Assessments

Regular audits and assessments provide deeper insights into a supplier's operational capabilities, compliance, and adherence to agreed standards. These evaluations can be conducted on-site or remotely and may cover areas such as production processes, quality control measures, and labor practices. Supplier audits are especially critical in industries with stringent regulatory requirements, such as pharmaceuticals and aerospace.

Feedback and Communication

Open and transparent communication between buyers and suppliers is essential for effective SPM. Regular feedback sessions enable suppliers to understand their strengths and areas for improvement. Constructive feedback fosters collaboration and helps suppliers align their operations with the buyer's expectations.

Corrective Action Plans (CAPs)

When performance gaps are identified, corrective action plans are implemented to address the root causes. CAPs outline specific steps the supplier must take to improve performance within a defined timeline. Progress is monitored through follow-up evaluations to ensure accountability and effectiveness.

Incentives and Recognition

Recognizing and rewarding high-performing suppliers can motivate continuous improvement and strengthen relationships. Incentives may include preferred supplier status, long-term contracts, or financial bonuses tied to performance metrics. Recognition fosters goodwill and encourages suppliers to exceed expectations.

The Role of Technology in SPM

Technology has transformed supplier performance management by automating data collection, analysis, and reporting. Advanced tools such as supplier management software, artificial intelligence (AI), and blockchain enable organizations to manage supplier relationships more efficiently and transparently.

Supplier Management Software

Supplier management platforms integrate various aspects of SPM, from KPI tracking to contract management. These tools provide real-time insights into supplier performance, enabling data-driven decision-making.

AI and Predictive Analytics

AI-driven analytics identify performance trends, predict potential risks, and suggest corrective actions. For example, predictive models can forecast delays based on historical data, allowing organizations to proactively address issues.

Blockchain for Transparency

Blockchain technology enhances transparency and traceability in supplier relationships. It enables secure and immutable records of transactions, certifications, and compliance, reducing the risk of fraud or misrepresentation.

Challenges in Supplier Performance Management

Despite its benefits, SPM presents several challenges that organizations must address to maximize its effectiveness.

Data Quality and Consistency

Poor-quality or inconsistent data can undermine the accuracy of performance evaluations. Organizations must invest in robust data collection and validation processes to ensure reliability.

Resistance from Suppliers

Suppliers may resist SPM initiatives, perceiving them as overly intrusive or burdensome. Building trust and communicating the mutual benefits of SPM are essential to overcoming resistance.

Resource Constraints

Implementing and maintaining an effective SPM system requires resources, including skilled personnel and technology investments. Smaller organizations may face constraints in allocating these resources.

Dynamic Market Conditions

Rapid changes in market conditions, such as economic downturns or supply chain disruptions, can impact supplier performance. Organizations must adapt their SPM strategies to account for such volatility.

Benefits of Effective Supplier Performance Management

When implemented effectively, SPM delivers significant benefits that extend beyond operational efficiency.

Enhanced Quality and Reliability

SPM ensures that suppliers consistently deliver high-quality products or services, reducing rework, returns, and customer complaints.

Cost Optimization

By identifying inefficiencies and negotiating better terms, organizations can achieve significant cost savings without compromising quality.

Stronger Supplier Relationships

SPM fosters trust and collaboration, transforming transactional relationships into strategic partnerships that deliver long-term value.

Improved Risk Management

Proactive monitoring and mitigation of risks enhance supply chain resilience, minimizing disruptions and financial losses.

Alignment with Strategic Goals

By aligning supplier performance with organizational objectives, SPM drives overall business success and competitive advantage.

Conclusion

Supplier performance management is a cornerstone of modern procurement and supply chain strategy. It combines objective evaluation, continuous improvement, and collaborative engagement to ensure that suppliers meet the organization's expectations. By leveraging advanced tools and fostering strong relationships, organizations can optimize supplier performance, mitigate risks, and achieve sustainable growth. For professionals in procurement, mastering SPM is not just a technical skill but a strategic imperative that directly impacts the success of the broader supply chain.

Chapter 6: Strategic Sourcing

Strategic Sourcing: Definition and Process

Strategic sourcing is a comprehensive and proactive approach to procurement that seeks to align an organization's purchasing activities with its overarching business goals. It transcends the traditional view of procurement as a transactional function and focuses on creating long-term value by optimizing costs, improving supplier relationships, and fostering innovation. As global competition intensifies and supply chains grow more complex, strategic sourcing has become a critical tool for organizations aiming to remain agile, efficient, and competitive.

Definition of Strategic Sourcing

At its core, strategic sourcing is the process of analyzing an organization's procurement spend and aligning it with strategic objectives. It involves a deliberate and data-driven approach to selecting, managing, and collaborating with suppliers. Unlike tactical purchasing, which emphasizes immediate needs and short-term solutions, strategic sourcing considers the broader implications of procurement decisions, including cost structures, supplier capabilities, market trends, and risk factors.

Strategic sourcing is not merely about obtaining the lowest price; it focuses on achieving the best total value. This means considering quality, service, sustainability, innovation potential, and long-term partnership opportunities in addition to cost. By emphasizing strategic alignment, organizations can ensure their sourcing activities directly contribute to competitive advantage and operational excellence.

The Strategic Sourcing Process

The strategic sourcing process is systematic and iterative, typically encompassing several key stages. These stages ensure that sourcing decisions are informed by data, aligned with business goals, and adaptable to changing market conditions. While specific methodologies may vary across industries and organizations, the fundamental principles of the process remain consistent.

Spend Analysis

The first step in strategic sourcing is conducting a thorough spend analysis. This involves examining the organization's procurement expenditures to identify patterns, opportunities, and inefficiencies. By categorizing spend data by supplier, product category, geographic region, and other dimensions, organizations can gain insights into their purchasing behavior and highlight areas for improvement.

Spend analysis often reveals opportunities for cost savings, such as consolidating suppliers, renegotiating contracts, or standardizing purchases. It also helps identify critical spend categories that require strategic focus, such as high-value or high-risk suppliers.

Market Research and Supplier Analysis

Understanding the supply market is essential for making informed sourcing decisions. Market research involves evaluating the dynamics of the industry or sector in which suppliers operate, including trends, competitive pressures, technological advancements, and regulatory considerations.

Supplier analysis is an extension of this research, focusing on assessing the capabilities, strengths, weaknesses, and potential of current and prospective suppliers. Factors such as financial stability, production capacity, geographical reach, and innovation capabilities are critical in determining a supplier's suitability for strategic partnerships.

Defining Sourcing Objectives and Strategy

Once spend patterns and market dynamics are understood, organizations define their sourcing objectives and develop a strategy to achieve them. These objectives are guided by broader business goals, such as cost reduction, quality enhancement, risk mitigation, or sustainability.

For example, an organization prioritizing sustainability may seek suppliers with robust environmental practices and certifications. Conversely, a company focused on cost leadership may prioritize suppliers with economies of scale and competitive pricing.

The sourcing strategy outlines the criteria for supplier selection, the desired mix of global versus local suppliers, and the balance between single-source and multi-source approaches. It also establishes key performance indicators (KPIs) to measure the success of the sourcing initiative.

Supplier Selection and Negotiation

The next step in the process is selecting suppliers that align with the defined objectives and strategy. This involves issuing requests for information (RFIs), requests for proposals (RFPs), or requests for quotations (RFQs) to gather detailed insights from potential suppliers.

Evaluation of supplier responses is typically based on a combination of quantitative and qualitative criteria, such as pricing, quality, delivery performance, and alignment with organizational values. Strategic sourcing teams may use weighted scoring models to objectively compare suppliers and facilitate decision-making.

Negotiation is a critical component of supplier selection, aiming to establish mutually beneficial terms. Effective negotiation focuses not only on price but also on value-added factors such as service levels, innovation contributions, risk-sharing mechanisms, and long-term partnership frameworks.

Contracting and Implementation

Once suppliers are selected and terms are negotiated, contracts are formalized. Strategic sourcing contracts often include detailed specifications, performance expectations, dispute resolution mechanisms, and provisions for regular reviews. Contracts serve as a foundation for the relationship, providing clarity and accountability for both parties.

Implementation involves integrating the selected suppliers into the organization's operations and systems. This may include onboarding processes, establishing communication channels, and aligning logistics and supply chain workflows.

Performance Monitoring and Continuous Improvement

Strategic sourcing is not a one-time activity; it requires ongoing monitoring and continuous improvement. Performance monitoring ensures that suppliers meet their contractual obligations and KPIs. Regular performance reviews and audits help identify areas for improvement and maintain alignment with organizational objectives.

Continuous improvement is a hallmark of strategic sourcing. Organizations work collaboratively with suppliers to innovate, enhance efficiency, and address emerging challenges. By fostering a culture of partnership and adaptability, strategic sourcing drives sustained value creation.

The Strategic Role of Technology

Technology plays a pivotal role in enabling and enhancing the strategic sourcing process. Advanced tools and platforms streamline data collection, analysis, and collaboration, making sourcing decisions more informed and efficient.

Spend Management Software

Spend management software provides visibility into procurement data, enabling organizations to identify trends, optimize spending, and uncover cost-saving opportunities. These tools integrate with enterprise resource planning (ERP) systems to provide real-time insights and analytics.

E-Sourcing Platforms

E-sourcing platforms facilitate supplier communication, RFP/RFQ processes, and bid evaluations. By automating these activities, organizations can reduce administrative burdens and accelerate decision-making.

Supplier Relationship Management (SRM) Tools

SRM tools support the ongoing management and evaluation of supplier relationships. These platforms provide dashboards, scorecards, and collaboration features that enhance transparency and foster partnership.

Artificial Intelligence and Predictive Analytics

AI and predictive analytics are increasingly used in strategic sourcing to forecast market trends, assess supplier risks, and recommend optimal sourcing strategies. These technologies enable organizations to stay ahead of industry changes and proactively address potential disruptions.

Challenges in Strategic Sourcing

Despite its benefits, strategic sourcing presents several challenges that organizations must navigate.

Data Quality and Integration

Accurate and comprehensive data is essential for effective strategic sourcing. However, many organizations struggle with fragmented or inconsistent data across systems and departments. Ensuring data quality and integration requires investment in technology and process improvements.

Supplier Resistance to Collaboration

Not all suppliers are receptive to strategic sourcing initiatives, especially if they perceive them as overly demanding or restrictive. Building trust and demonstrating mutual value are critical to overcoming resistance and fostering collaboration.

Market Volatility

Rapid changes in market conditions, such as economic downturns, geopolitical tensions, or supply chain disruptions, can impact sourcing strategies. Organizations must remain agile and adapt their approaches to mitigate risks and capitalize on opportunities.

Balancing Cost and Value

Striking the right balance between cost efficiency and long-term value creation is a perennial challenge in strategic sourcing. Overemphasis on cost reduction can lead to compromised quality or strained supplier relationships.

The Benefits of Strategic Sourcing

When executed effectively, strategic sourcing delivers significant benefits that extend across the organization.

Cost Optimization

Strategic sourcing reduces procurement costs through smarter supplier selection, negotiation, and spend management. Cost savings are achieved without sacrificing quality or service levels.

Improved Supplier Relationships

By fostering collaboration and trust, strategic sourcing strengthens relationships with key suppliers. These partnerships drive innovation, enhance efficiency, and provide a foundation for mutual success.

Risk Mitigation

Strategic sourcing identifies and addresses potential risks, such as supplier insolvency, regulatory non-compliance, or supply chain disruptions. Proactive risk management enhances supply chain resilience and operational stability.

Alignment with Business Goals

Strategic sourcing aligns procurement activities with broader organizational objectives, ensuring that sourcing decisions support growth, sustainability, and competitive advantage.

Conclusion

Strategic sourcing represents a transformative approach to procurement, elevating it from a transactional function to a strategic enabler of business success. By focusing on data-driven decision-making, supplier collaboration, and continuous improvement, organizations can unlock significant value and maintain a competitive edge in an increasingly dynamic marketplace. For professionals in procurement and supply chain management, mastering strategic sourcing is essential to driving innovation, efficiency, and long-term growth.

Total Cost of Ownership (TCO)

The concept of Total Cost of Ownership (TCO) has become a cornerstone in modern procurement and supply chain management, emphasizing a holistic approach to evaluating the costs associated with acquiring and using a product or service over its entire lifecycle. TCO extends beyond the purchase price, capturing the broader spectrum of costs that impact an organization's financial and operational performance. This approach provides organizations with a more comprehensive understanding of value, enabling better decision-making and fostering long-term sustainability.

Definition of Total Cost of Ownership

TCO is a financial metric used to evaluate the direct and indirect costs of purchasing, operating, and maintaining a product, service, or system throughout its lifecycle. It encompasses all expenditures incurred from acquisition to disposal, offering a complete picture of the true financial impact of procurement decisions. Unlike traditional cost analysis, which often focuses solely on upfront expenses, TCO considers hidden or downstream costs that can significantly affect the overall value proposition.

For instance, while a low-cost supplier may seem attractive initially, their products might lead to higher maintenance costs, reduced efficiency, or increased downtime over time. By considering TCO, organizations can weigh these trade-offs and make more informed choices.

Components of TCO

TCO comprises a wide range of cost elements, typically divided into three categories: acquisition costs, operating costs, and end-of-life costs. Each category contributes to the overall financial impact of a procurement decision.

Acquisition Costs

Acquisition costs are the direct expenses associated with procuring a product or service. These include:

Purchase Price: The actual cost of the item or service being procured.

Transportation and Logistics: Expenses related to shipping, handling, and delivering the product to its destination.

Installation and Implementation: Costs of setting up or integrating the product into existing systems or operations.

Taxes and Duties: Any applicable tariffs, import fees, or sales taxes.

While acquisition costs are the most visible component of TCO, they often represent only a fraction of the total costs incurred over the lifecycle of the product or service.

Operating Costs

Operating costs account for the expenses incurred during the use and maintenance of the product or service. These include:

Maintenance and Repairs: Costs for regular upkeep and addressing unexpected issues.

Energy Consumption: Utility expenses for operating equipment or systems, particularly relevant for energy-intensive machinery.

Training: Costs of educating staff on the proper use or maintenance of the product.

Downtime and Productivity Losses: Financial impact of disruptions caused by equipment failure or inefficiencies.

Operating costs often exceed acquisition costs over time, making them a critical consideration in TCO analysis.

End-of-Life Costs

End-of-life costs are associated with the disposal or replacement of a product or service. These include:

Disposal and Recycling: Expenses related to safely discarding or recycling the product.

Decommissioning: Costs of removing or dismantling equipment or systems.

Resale Value: Potential revenue from selling the product at the end of its useful life.

Understanding end-of-life costs is essential for sustainable procurement practices, as improper disposal can lead to environmental and regulatory penalties.

The Role of TCO in Procurement Decisions

TCO plays a vital role in procurement by shifting the focus from short-term cost savings to long-term value creation. By evaluating all cost elements, organizations can make more strategic choices that align with their financial, operational, and sustainability goals.

Vendor Selection

TCO analysis helps organizations select suppliers that offer the best overall value rather than the lowest upfront price. For example, a supplier with higher initial costs but lower operating and maintenance expenses may ultimately provide greater value over the lifecycle of the product.

Budgeting and Forecasting

By accounting for all cost components, TCO enables more accurate budgeting and financial planning. Organizations can anticipate future expenses and allocate resources effectively, reducing the risk of unexpected financial burdens.

Risk Mitigation

TCO analysis identifies potential cost drivers and risks, such as high maintenance expenses or frequent downtime. This insight allows organizations to address vulnerabilities and enhance supply chain resilience.

Sustainability Initiatives

TCO supports sustainability by incorporating environmental and social costs into procurement decisions. For instance, choosing energy-efficient equipment may have higher upfront costs but result in significant savings on energy consumption and reduced environmental impact over time.

Challenges in TCO Analysis

While TCO offers numerous benefits, its implementation can be complex and challenging. Common obstacles include:

Data Availability and Accuracy

Accurate TCO analysis requires comprehensive data on all cost elements, which may not always be readily available. Organizations often face difficulties in tracking indirect or hidden costs, such as downtime or training expenses.

Complexity of Calculations

TCO calculations can be intricate, particularly for products or services with long lifecycles or variable costs. This complexity may deter organizations from adopting TCO as a standard practice.

Resistance to Change

Stakeholders accustomed to focusing on upfront costs may resist adopting a TCO perspective. Overcoming this resistance requires education and demonstrating the value of a lifecycle approach.

Strategies for Effective TCO Implementation

Organizations can overcome these challenges and leverage TCO effectively by adopting the following strategies:

Invest in Technology and Tools

Advanced analytics tools and procurement software can simplify TCO calculations by automating data collection, analysis, and reporting. These tools provide real-time insights and support data-driven decision-making.

Engage Stakeholders

Engaging stakeholders across departments, including finance, operations, and sustainability, ensures a holistic approach to TCO analysis. Collaboration fosters alignment and buy-in for TCO-based decisions.

Educate and Train Teams

Providing training on the principles and benefits of TCO helps build awareness and expertise within the organization. Training programs should emphasize practical applications and case studies to demonstrate real-world impact.

Adopt Standardized Frameworks

Standardized frameworks and methodologies for TCO analysis ensure consistency and comparability across procurement decisions. Organizations can develop internal guidelines or adopt industry standards to streamline the process.

The Future of TCO in Procurement

As organizations face growing pressures to reduce costs, enhance sustainability, and navigate complex supply chains, the importance of

TCO will continue to rise. Advances in technology, such as artificial intelligence and blockchain, are expected to further enhance TCO analysis by providing more accurate data, predictive insights, and transparency.

Moreover, the integration of TCO with broader strategic initiatives, such as sustainability reporting and risk management, will solidify its role as a critical tool in modern procurement. By embracing TCO, organizations can achieve a more comprehensive understanding of value, drive long-term success, and maintain a competitive edge in an increasingly dynamic marketplace.

Conclusion

Total Cost of Ownership is a transformative concept that redefines the way organizations evaluate procurement decisions. By considering all lifecycle costs, TCO shifts the focus from short-term price savings to long-term value creation. Despite its challenges, TCO offers significant benefits in terms of cost optimization, risk mitigation, and sustainability. For professionals in procurement and supply chain management, mastering TCO is essential for driving strategic decision-making and achieving operational excellence.

Risk Management in Sourcing

Risk management in sourcing is a critical function in modern procurement and supply chain management, where globalized operations and interconnected networks create an environment rife with potential disruptions. Effective risk management ensures that sourcing activities are not only efficient but also resilient, capable of withstanding and adapting to uncertainties and challenges. By proactively identifying, analyzing, and mitigating risks, organizations safeguard their operations, maintain continuity, and secure long-term strategic objectives.

The Importance of Risk Management in Sourcing

Sourcing involves procuring goods, services, or materials required for business operations, often from a complex network of suppliers. This complexity introduces risks that can arise from economic fluctuations, geopolitical instability, supplier failures, or natural disasters. The COVID-19 pandemic, for example, underscored the vulnerabilities in sourcing networks, with widespread supply chain disruptions that highlighted the necessity of robust risk management strategies.

For organizations, unmanaged sourcing risks can result in production delays, increased costs, reputational damage, and even legal repercussions. Risk management in sourcing, therefore, is essential not only for operational efficiency but also for maintaining competitive advantage and protecting brand equity.

Types of Risks in Sourcing

Risks in sourcing can be broadly categorized into several domains, each with unique challenges and implications. Understanding these risks is the first step in developing effective mitigation strategies.

Supply Chain Disruptions

Disruptions to the supply chain, such as transportation delays, port congestions, or raw material shortages, can halt operations and affect delivery timelines. These disruptions are often caused by unforeseen events like natural disasters, strikes, or pandemics.

Supplier Reliability

The reliability and performance of suppliers play a crucial role in sourcing success. Risks include supplier insolvency, quality failures, or inability to meet contractual obligations. Over-reliance on a single supplier or region further exacerbates this risk.

Geopolitical and Economic Risks

Sourcing from global suppliers exposes organizations to geopolitical risks, such as trade wars, sanctions, or regulatory changes. Economic factors like currency fluctuations and inflation also impact the cost and feasibility of sourcing arrangements.

Compliance and Legal Risks

Non-compliance with regulatory standards or ethical guidelines can lead to fines, legal actions, and reputational harm. This risk is particularly relevant in industries with stringent safety or environmental regulations.

Technological and Cyber Risks

The increasing reliance on digital platforms for procurement introduces risks related to data breaches, system outages, and cyberattacks. These risks can compromise sensitive supplier information and disrupt sourcing activities.

Environmental and Social Risks

Sourcing activities that harm the environment or violate social standards, such as labor rights, can lead to reputational damage and regulatory penalties. Consumers and stakeholders are increasingly holding organizations accountable for sustainable and ethical sourcing practices.

The Process of Risk Management in Sourcing

Effective risk management in sourcing follows a structured process, enabling organizations to systematically address potential challenges.

Risk Identification

The first step in managing sourcing risks is to identify potential threats across the supply chain. This involves assessing supplier capabilities, geopolitical conditions, market trends, and operational vulnerabilities. Risk mapping tools and frameworks, such as the Risk Breakdown Structure (RBS), can aid in this process.

Risk Assessment and Prioritization

Once risks are identified, they must be analyzed in terms of their likelihood and potential impact. Quantitative methods, such as risk matrices or probabilistic modeling, help prioritize risks that pose the greatest threat to sourcing activities.

Risk Mitigation Strategies

Mitigating sourcing risks involves implementing measures to reduce their likelihood or impact. Strategies include diversifying the supplier base, negotiating flexible contracts, and investing in supply chain visibility tools. Contingency planning, such as maintaining safety stock or identifying alternative suppliers, is also crucial.

Monitoring and Review

Risk management is an ongoing process that requires continuous monitoring and periodic reviews. Key risk indicators (KRIs) and dashboards provide real-time insights into emerging threats, enabling organizations to adapt their strategies proactively.

Best Practices in Sourcing Risk Management

Adopting best practices ensures that risk management efforts are comprehensive and effective. These practices align sourcing strategies with broader organizational goals, fostering resilience and agility.

Supplier Diversification

Relying on a single supplier or geographic region increases vulnerability to disruptions. Diversifying the supplier base and sourcing from multiple locations reduces dependency and enhances flexibility.

Collaboration and Communication

Strong relationships with suppliers are essential for risk management. Open communication and collaboration enable organizations to identify potential issues early and work together to develop solutions.

Technology Adoption

Digital tools, such as predictive analytics, blockchain, and supplier relationship management (SRM) systems, enhance risk management capabilities. These technologies provide real-time data, improve transparency, and streamline decision-making.

Ethical and Sustainable Sourcing

Incorporating ethical and sustainability criteria into sourcing decisions mitigates environmental and social risks. Certifications, audits, and partnerships with responsible suppliers reinforce commitment to corporate social responsibility (CSR) goals.

Scenario Planning and Simulation

Scenario planning involves exploring hypothetical situations and assessing their impact on sourcing activities. This practice helps organizations prepare for a range of potential risks and develop adaptive strategies.

The Role of Leadership in Risk Management

Leadership plays a pivotal role in embedding risk management into sourcing activities. By fostering a culture of risk awareness, leaders ensure that risk considerations are integrated into decision-making processes. Effective leaders prioritize investments in risk management tools and training, empowering teams to navigate uncertainties with confidence.

Case Studies in Sourcing Risk Management

Examining real-world examples illustrates the importance of proactive risk management in sourcing.

Apple Inc. and Supplier Resilience

Apple's supply chain strategy includes diversifying its supplier base and maintaining strong relationships with key partners. This approach helped the company mitigate risks during the COVID-19 pandemic, ensuring continued production and distribution of its products.

Unilever and Sustainable Sourcing

Unilever's commitment to sustainable sourcing minimizes environmental and social risks. By working closely with certified suppliers and adhering to strict sustainability standards, the company enhances its reputation while mitigating long-term risks.

Future Trends in Sourcing Risk Management

The field of sourcing risk management is evolving, with emerging trends shaping its future.

Artificial Intelligence and Machine Learning

AI and machine learning enable predictive risk modeling, providing organizations with early warnings of potential disruptions. These technologies enhance decision-making and support proactive risk mitigation.

Blockchain for Transparency

Blockchain technology ensures transparency and traceability in sourcing activities. By securely recording transactions, organizations can verify supplier compliance and mitigate risks related to fraud or counterfeiting.

Focus on Resilience

The increasing frequency of global disruptions has shifted the focus from cost efficiency to resilience. Organizations are investing in strategies that enhance their ability to adapt and recover from unexpected events.

Risk management in sourcing is a critical component of modern procurement and supply chain strategies. By identifying, assessing, and mitigating risks, organizations can protect their operations, reduce costs, and maintain competitiveness. Adopting best practices, leveraging technology, and fostering collaboration with suppliers ensure that risk management efforts are effective and aligned with organizational goals. In an increasingly uncertain world, robust risk management in sourcing is not just a necessity—it is a strategic advantage.

Chapter 7: Negotiation and Contract Management

Principles of Effective Negotiation

Negotiation is an essential skill in procurement and supply chain management, playing a pivotal role in ensuring that organizations achieve favorable terms in their contracts with suppliers, partners, and other stakeholders. In this context, effective negotiation goes beyond simply reaching an agreement. It requires a strategic approach, emotional intelligence, and the ability to create value for all parties involved. In supply chain management, negotiations are often complex, involving multiple factors such as pricing, delivery terms, quality standards, and timelines. The principles of effective negotiation are therefore crucial for procurement professionals who seek to optimize value, minimize risk, and maintain strong business relationships.

Understanding the Importance of Negotiation in Procurement

Negotiation is the process of discussing and reaching a mutual agreement between two or more parties with differing needs or viewpoints. In procurement, effective negotiation ensures that organizations get the best value for their money while securing high-quality goods and services. It is not just about price reduction, but also about negotiating favorable terms, understanding supplier capabilities, and aligning goals with strategic objectives. A successful negotiation can lead to reduced costs, improved supplier performance, enhanced supply chain resilience, and long-term business partnerships.

The importance of negotiation extends beyond the immediate transaction. The ability to negotiate effectively helps build trust, mitigate risks, and ensure that both parties have a clear understanding of their responsibilities and expectations. As the supply chain landscape becomes increasingly global and interconnected, strong negotiation skills are essential to managing the complexities of international trade, compliance regulations, and geopolitical uncertainties.

Key Principles of Effective Negotiation

Effective negotiation is guided by several core principles that help ensure that outcomes are beneficial, sustainable, and aligned with both parties' interests. These principles are essential for procurement professionals who need to balance cost reduction with quality and relationship management.

Preparation is Key

One of the most important principles in any negotiation is thorough preparation. Negotiations rarely succeed when conducted without adequate knowledge of the other party's position, industry standards, and the potential challenges that may arise. Preparation involves researching the supplier's financial health, understanding their capabilities, and identifying their needs. In addition, it is crucial to understand the internal requirements of the organization, including budget constraints, quality expectations, and delivery timelines.

A well-prepared negotiator also anticipates potential objections and prepares responses in advance. This proactive approach enables negotiators to stay calm, composed, and adaptable throughout the negotiation process. Moreover, understanding the underlying interests and motivations of the other party can provide valuable insights into potential solutions and compromises.

Creating Win-Win Outcomes

In effective negotiation, both parties should feel that they have gained something valuable from the agreement. This approach fosters long-term relationships, trust, and collaboration. Instead of focusing solely on securing the lowest price, successful negotiators aim to create win-win solutions by identifying areas where both sides can benefit.

For example, a supplier may be willing to offer better pricing in exchange for longer contract durations or a commitment to larger order volumes. Similarly, procurement professionals may negotiate for value-added services, such as better delivery terms or enhanced product features, in addition to competitive pricing. By focusing on creating mutual value, both parties are more likely to come away from the negotiation with a sense of accomplishment and a stronger foundation for future collaboration.

Effective Communication

Communication is at the heart of every negotiation. Whether it is verbal or non-verbal, clear and effective communication enables negotiators to convey their needs, interests, and positions in a way that the other party can understand. Active listening is a crucial component of communication, as it helps negotiators gather important information, demonstrate empathy, and build rapport.

Negotiators should aim to be concise and precise when articulating their points. This clarity helps avoid misunderstandings and ensures that both parties are on the same page. It is equally important to be mindful of body language, tone, and facial expressions, as these non-verbal cues can convey confidence, openness, or resistance.

Building Trust and Rapport

Trust is a fundamental element of effective negotiation. Without trust, negotiations can become adversarial, with each party trying to protect their own interests at the expense of the other. Establishing trust helps create an environment where both parties are more likely to engage in open, honest communication and work towards mutually beneficial outcomes.

Building rapport is a key strategy in establishing trust. This can be achieved by demonstrating respect for the other party, acknowledging their concerns, and finding common ground. Small gestures, such as recognizing the other party's achievements or acknowledging their expertise, can go a long way in creating a positive atmosphere for negotiation. Trust and rapport also help to diffuse potential conflicts, enabling negotiators to handle disagreements constructively.

Flexibility and Adaptability

Negotiation is rarely a linear process, and effective negotiators must be flexible and adaptable in their approach. Circumstances, priorities, and perspectives often change during the course of a negotiation, and successful negotiators are those who can adjust their strategies and tactics accordingly.

This adaptability involves being open to alternative solutions and recognizing when it may be necessary to modify one's position to reach a favorable outcome. While it is important to be clear about non-negotiable terms, being rigid on every issue can lead to deadlock and a failure to reach an agreement. Flexibility is particularly important in complex negotiations, where unexpected challenges may arise, and new solutions must be explored.

Understanding Power Dynamics

In any negotiation, there is an inherent power dynamic that can influence the outcome. Understanding the sources of power—whether it is market knowledge, financial resources, or the ability to walk away from the deal—allows negotiators to position themselves strategically. However, effective negotiators recognize that power should not be used as a tool for domination but rather as a means to leverage value for both parties.

In some cases, power may shift during the negotiation, with one party gaining an upper hand due to a new revelation or change in circumstances. Skilled negotiators are able to navigate these shifts in power while maintaining a collaborative mindset. This means that they do not rely solely on their power but seek to create balanced solutions that benefit both parties.

Negotiating on Interests, Not Positions

One of the most important principles in negotiation is focusing on underlying interests rather than fixed positions. Often, negotiators become entrenched in their positions, such as insisting on a specific price or delivery schedule. However, positions are usually reflective of underlying needs or desires, which can be more flexible.

By probing for the underlying interests of both parties, negotiators can identify areas for compromise and creative solutions. For example, a supplier may demand higher prices due to increased production costs, but their underlying interest may be a stable, long-term partnership with predictable demand. By focusing on interests, procurement professionals can find ways to meet both their organization's needs and the supplier's concerns.

Managing Emotions

Negotiation can evoke strong emotions, such as frustration, excitement, or even anger. These emotions can cloud judgment and hinder effective communication. Skilled negotiators recognize the importance of emotional intelligence—being aware of their own emotions as well as those of the other party.

Maintaining emotional control allows negotiators to respond thoughtfully rather than react impulsively. It is important to remain calm and professional, even when the negotiation becomes tense or contentious. Acknowledging emotions—both positive and negative—can also help to build rapport and address underlying concerns in a constructive manner.

Ethical Negotiation

Ethical behavior is essential in negotiation. Procurement professionals must ensure that their negotiation tactics are fair, transparent, and in line with the organization's ethical standards. This includes avoiding deceptive practices, honoring agreements, and respecting confidentiality. Ethical negotiation builds long-term trust and enhances the organization's reputation, while unethical tactics can lead to legal ramifications and damaged relationships.

The principles of effective negotiation are essential for procurement professionals who seek to secure favorable terms, foster strong supplier relationships, and create value for their organizations. Successful negotiation is not just about achieving the lowest price; it is about understanding the needs and interests of both parties, maintaining flexibility, and finding mutually beneficial solutions. With preparation, effective communication, trust, and adaptability, procurement professionals can navigate the complexities of negotiations and drive success in sourcing and contract management. As the global business environment continues to evolve, the ability to negotiate effectively remains a critical skill for procurement leaders striving to optimize value, reduce risk, and strengthen supply chain partnerships.

Types of Procurement Contracts

In procurement and supply chain management, contracts serve as the legal framework for the relationship between the buyer and the supplier. These contracts define the terms and conditions under which goods and services are provided, ensuring that both parties are aligned with expectations, responsibilities, and deliverables. Understanding the different types of procurement contracts is crucial for procurement professionals as each type offers distinct advantages and challenges, depending on the specific project or business needs.

Procurement contracts are generally classified based on the structure of the agreement and the manner in which the price or compensation is determined. These contracts can be broadly categorized into four main types: **fixed-price contracts**, **cost-reimbursement contracts**, **time and materials contracts**, and **incentive-based contracts**. Each type of contract is designed to meet specific procurement objectives, provide flexibility, and manage risk in different ways.

Fixed-Price Contracts

A fixed-price contract is the most straightforward and commonly used type of procurement contract. As the name suggests, the price is agreed upon at the outset of the contract and remains unchanged throughout its duration, regardless of any fluctuations in the cost of materials, labor, or other factors. Fixed-price contracts are typically used when the scope of work and deliverables are clearly defined, and both parties are confident that the price can be accurately determined.

Advantages of Fixed-Price Contracts

One of the key advantages of fixed-price contracts is cost predictability. Since the price is set in advance, the buyer knows exactly what they will be paying for the goods or services provided, which helps in budgeting and financial planning. This type of contract also shifts the risk of cost overruns to the supplier, as they are responsible for any unforeseen expenses. Fixed-price contracts also provide a clear incentive for suppliers to complete the work efficiently and on time, as they are not compensated for any delays or cost overruns.

Challenges of Fixed-Price Contracts

However, fixed-price contracts may not always be suitable for projects that involve a high degree of uncertainty or where the scope of work is not fully defined. If there are changes in requirements or unforeseen challenges arise, suppliers may be reluctant to absorb the additional costs, potentially leading to disputes. Furthermore, while the buyer is protected from cost increases, they may not always get the best quality or service if the supplier cuts corners to maintain profitability.

Cost-Reimbursement Contracts

Cost-reimbursement contracts, also known as cost-plus contracts, are a type of agreement where the buyer reimburses the supplier for the actual costs incurred during the execution of the contract, in addition to a fixed fee or percentage for profit. These contracts are commonly used for projects where the scope of work is difficult to define upfront or when the work is likely to evolve over time, making it difficult to estimate a fixed price.

Advantages of Cost-Reimbursement Contracts

Cost-reimbursement contracts offer flexibility and are well-suited for complex or research and development projects where the requirements may change as work progresses. Since the supplier is reimbursed for all allowable costs, they are not financially at risk for unforeseen expenses. This can lead to a more collaborative relationship between the buyer and supplier, as both parties share the burden of risk in the project.

Challenges of Cost-Reimbursement Contracts

One of the primary disadvantages of cost-reimbursement contracts is the lack of cost predictability. The buyer may be exposed to higher costs than initially anticipated, especially if the scope of work expands or if the supplier's costs are higher than expected. To mitigate this risk, the buyer may include a cap on the total amount reimbursed, but this still requires close monitoring of costs throughout the project. Additionally, there is less incentive for suppliers to control costs since they are reimbursed for all expenses, which can result in inefficiencies or overcharging.

Time and Materials Contracts

Time and materials (T&M) contracts are a hybrid form of procurement agreement that combines elements of both fixed-price and cost-reimbursement contracts. Under a T&M contract, the buyer agrees to pay the supplier based on the time spent working on the project and the materials used. The rates for labor and materials are typically agreed upon at the outset, but the overall cost is determined by the actual time and resources required to complete the work.

Advantages of Time and Materials Contracts

Time and materials contracts are beneficial when the scope of work is uncertain or difficult to define, making it challenging to agree on a fixed price. They provide flexibility and allow the project to evolve as new requirements emerge. This type of contract is often used for services or projects where the buyer needs expertise on an ongoing basis but is not able to predict the exact number of hours required. Additionally, T&M contracts provide a clear breakdown of costs, which can help the buyer monitor and control spending more effectively.

Challenges of Time and Materials Contracts

The main drawback of T&M contracts is the potential for cost escalation. Since the buyer is paying for both time and materials, there is less control over the final cost. The supplier may be incentivized to take longer or use more materials than necessary, leading to higher costs for the buyer. As a result, close monitoring of the project is essential to ensure that work progresses efficiently and within budget.

Incentive-Based Contracts

Incentive-based contracts, also known as performance-based contracts, are designed to encourage suppliers to complete the project ahead of schedule, under budget, or with higher quality than required. These contracts typically include a base price or payment that is adjusted based on the supplier's performance in meeting specific goals or objectives, such as early delivery, cost savings, or high-quality standards.

Advantages of Incentive-Based Contracts

Incentive-based contracts are effective in aligning the interests of both the buyer and supplier. By linking compensation to performance, suppliers are motivated to work more efficiently, reduce costs, and improve the quality of the goods or services provided. This type of contract fosters collaboration between the buyer and supplier, as both parties are incentivized to achieve the best possible outcomes. Additionally, buyers can share in the savings or benefits derived from improved performance, which can lead to a more cost-effective and successful project.

Challenges of Incentive-Based Contracts

While incentive-based contracts offer the potential for improved performance, they can be challenging to implement. Defining clear, measurable performance criteria and ensuring that both parties agree on the terms is crucial. There is also the risk that the supplier may focus on meeting specific performance targets at the expense of other important factors, such as long-term quality or sustainability. In some cases, suppliers may also game the system by exploiting loopholes to achieve the targets without truly adding value.

Other Types of Procurement Contracts

In addition to the four main types of contracts discussed above, there are several other variations that may be used in specific procurement scenarios:

> **Framework Agreements**: These are long-term contracts between a buyer and a supplier that set out the terms and conditions for future transactions. Framework agreements are commonly used when there is a need for a consistent supply of goods or services over an extended period. The specific details of each order, such as quantity and price, are determined at the time the order is placed.
>
> **Purchase Order Contracts**: A purchase order is a simple form of contract that details the buyer's requirements for goods or services. This is typically used for smaller, straightforward purchases, where the terms and conditions are simple and easily understood.

Joint Venture Contracts: In some cases, buyers and suppliers may enter into joint ventures, where both parties share risks, rewards, and responsibilities in the project. These contracts are often used for large-scale projects that require significant investment and expertise from both parties.

Each type of procurement contract offers distinct benefits and challenges, depending on the nature of the project, the relationship between the buyer and supplier, and the level of risk involved. Fixed-price contracts are best for projects with well-defined scopes, while cost-reimbursement contracts offer flexibility for more uncertain or evolving projects. Time and materials contracts provide a hybrid approach, while incentive-based contracts align the interests of both parties through performance-based compensation. Understanding the strengths and weaknesses of each contract type is essential for procurement professionals who must navigate complex procurement processes and negotiate favorable terms for their organizations. By selecting the appropriate type of contract for each situation, procurement professionals can mitigate risk, control costs, and foster strong supplier relationships.

Contract Lifecycle Management

Contract Lifecycle Management (CLM) refers to the process of managing contracts from the initial creation and negotiation stages through to execution, performance monitoring, and eventual renewal or termination. It involves the systematic and automated management of all stages of a contract's lifecycle, ensuring compliance, mitigating risks, and improving the overall efficiency and effectiveness of contract management within an organization. CLM is a critical aspect of procurement and supply chain management, as contracts serve as the foundation for business relationships, guiding expectations, responsibilities, and deliverables between parties.

The concept of CLM spans the entire duration of the contract, starting from its creation and negotiation to its execution, compliance management, performance evaluation, and post-contract activities such as amendments, renewals, or terminations. The implementation of effective CLM processes allows procurement professionals to streamline operations, reduce risks, optimize supplier relationships, and ensure that the terms of the contract are adhered to. By employing a structured CLM approach, organizations can maximize value, reduce costs, and minimize the potential for disputes or litigation.

Stages of Contract Lifecycle Management

Effective Contract Lifecycle Management encompasses several key stages. These stages form a structured approach to managing contracts, helping organizations maintain control over their contracts and optimize their procurement and supply chain activities.

1. Contract Creation

The lifecycle of any contract begins with the creation phase, where the contract's terms, conditions, and deliverables are negotiated and agreed upon. During this stage, procurement professionals must ensure that all necessary information, such as the scope of work, pricing, timelines, quality expectations, and legal clauses, is included in the draft contract. The creation phase also involves legal review to ensure that the contract complies with relevant laws and regulations, and that the terms adequately protect the interests of the organization.

Contract creation involves collaboration between various stakeholders, including legal teams, procurement officers, department heads, and sometimes external advisors. Technology can be employed at this stage to automate document creation and ensure consistency across contracts. Contract templates and clause libraries can be used to ensure that common terms and conditions are applied correctly and consistently, reducing errors and saving time.

2. Contract Negotiation

Once the draft contract is created, the negotiation phase begins. This stage is crucial in ensuring that both parties—buyer and supplier—are aligned on all terms, including price, delivery schedules, performance expectations, and dispute resolution mechanisms. Procurement professionals and legal teams typically lead the negotiation process, making sure that the terms protect the organization's interests while maintaining a positive working relationship with the supplier.

Negotiation often requires flexibility, as both parties may seek to adjust terms and conditions. The goal is to reach a mutually beneficial agreement that minimizes risks and clarifies the responsibilities of each party. Effective negotiation skills and a strong understanding of business needs and market conditions are critical at this stage. Additionally, advanced contract management software may be used to track changes and maintain version control to ensure that all parties have access to the most up-to-date version of the contract.

3. Contract Execution

Once both parties have agreed to the terms, the contract moves to the execution stage. This phase involves signing the contract and ensuring that all legal and regulatory requirements are met. The contract may be signed physically or digitally, depending on the organization's processes and the jurisdiction's legal requirements.

At this stage, it's important to ensure that all required signatures are obtained and that any preconditions, such as payment or regulatory filings, are fulfilled. Digital signatures and e-signature platforms can help streamline the execution process, ensuring that contracts are signed quickly and securely. Effective execution also requires that relevant departments and teams be notified that the contract is in place so that they can begin implementing the terms, such as placing purchase orders or initiating service delivery.

4. Contract Performance Monitoring

After execution, the focus shifts to performance monitoring, which is a critical part of Contract Lifecycle Management. During this phase, organizations must track the performance of the contract to ensure that both parties are adhering to the agreed-upon terms and conditions. This includes monitoring key performance indicators (KPIs) such as delivery schedules, product quality, service levels, and payment terms.

Regular communication with suppliers, along with periodic reviews of the contract's performance, is essential to ensure that any issues are identified and addressed in a timely manner. Non-compliance or deviations from contract terms can lead to disputes, delays, or additional costs, so early detection is crucial to mitigating these risks. Automated tools can assist in tracking milestones and deadlines, sending reminders for key actions, and generating reports to assess performance.

5. Contract Amendment and Renewal

Throughout the life of a contract, changes may arise due to shifts in market conditions, evolving business needs, or unforeseen circumstances. The contract amendment stage allows for modifications to the original agreement without the need to terminate it entirely. Amendments may include changes to the scope of work, delivery dates, pricing adjustments, or the introduction of new clauses to address unforeseen risks.

Similarly, as the contract nears its expiration date, the renewal phase begins. In some cases, contracts are automatically renewed, while in others, the organization must assess whether to continue with the supplier or seek alternatives. Contract renewal may require renegotiation of terms based on changing business requirements, supplier performance, or market conditions. It is essential to evaluate whether the contract continues to provide value and whether adjustments are needed before renewing it.

6. Contract Termination or Closeout

At the end of the contract's term, the final stage involves contract termination or closeout. This stage is initiated once all deliverables have been completed, and any outstanding obligations have been fulfilled by both parties. Contract closeout includes reviewing the contract to ensure that all terms and conditions have been met, that all payments have been made, and that no legal or financial issues remain outstanding.

If either party wishes to terminate the contract early, it is important to refer to the contract's termination clauses, which define the conditions under which the agreement can be ended before the completion date. Early termination may result in penalties or other consequences, so both parties must ensure that all terms are followed.

Once the contract has been completed or terminated, it is important to retain the contract documentation for future reference. The closeout process also includes conducting a post-mortem analysis to evaluate the overall performance of the contract. This analysis provides valuable insights into supplier performance, contract terms, and the effectiveness of the procurement process. Lessons learned during this phase can inform future procurement strategies and decision-making.

Benefits of Effective Contract Lifecycle Management

Implementing a robust Contract Lifecycle Management process brings several benefits to organizations. These benefits include:

> **Risk Mitigation**: By ensuring that contracts are properly created, negotiated, and managed, CLM helps mitigate legal and financial risks, including the risk of non-compliance, disputes, and contract breaches.
>
> **Cost Savings**: CLM enables organizations to identify cost-saving opportunities during negotiations, monitor supplier performance for potential discounts or penalties, and optimize the use of resources.

Improved Efficiency: By automating and streamlining contract creation, execution, and monitoring, CLM reduces manual effort, accelerates processes, and improves overall efficiency within procurement and legal teams.

Enhanced Supplier Relationships: A structured CLM process fosters transparency and accountability, promoting strong, long-term relationships with suppliers based on mutual trust and respect.

Data-Driven Insights: Effective CLM systems provide valuable data analytics that can help organizations assess supplier performance, track contract milestones, and make informed decisions about contract renewals or amendments.

Compliance and Auditability: CLM ensures that contracts comply with legal, regulatory, and internal standards. It also provides a complete audit trail, making it easier to track contract changes, approvals, and performance reviews.

Contract Lifecycle Management is a crucial function within procurement and supply chain management. By effectively managing the entire lifecycle of a contract, from creation through negotiation, execution, performance monitoring, and closeout, organizations can reduce risks, improve operational efficiency, and maximize value. Implementing a well-structured CLM process enhances the ability to manage complex contracts, track performance, and ensure compliance, while also fostering positive supplier relationships. As organizations continue to expand their procurement activities, the role of CLM will become increasingly important in ensuring that contracts align with business objectives and deliver long-term success.

Part 3: Advanced Supply Chain Management

Chapter 8: Demand Planning and Forecasting

Role of Demand Planning in the Supply Chain

Demand planning is one of the most critical aspects of effective supply chain management, ensuring that the right products are available at the right time and in the right quantities. It involves the process of forecasting future customer demand, aligning it with production and procurement activities, and ensuring that the supply chain can meet these needs. Demand planning is not merely a reactive process, where planners simply respond to market conditions; it is proactive and strategic, requiring an understanding of both short-term and long-term market trends, customer behavior, and organizational capabilities.

In the modern supply chain, demand planning plays a central role in bridging the gap between customer demand and supply chain operations. Its importance is not only in helping organizations optimize inventory levels and reduce costs, but also in improving customer satisfaction by ensuring product availability, minimizing stockouts, and avoiding excess inventory. Effective demand planning also ensures that production and procurement processes are aligned with actual customer requirements, avoiding waste, and improving overall supply chain efficiency.

Connecting Demand Planning with Overall Supply Chain Strategy

The relationship between demand planning and the overall supply chain strategy is crucial. An organization's ability to meet customer demand depends on how well its supply chain is designed and how accurately it can predict that demand. Without effective demand planning, companies risk understocking, which can lead to missed sales and dissatisfied customers, or overstocking, which results in higher holding costs, potential waste, and inefficiencies in the supply chain.

Demand planning is integrated with many other areas of supply chain management, such as procurement, inventory management, production scheduling, and logistics. By aligning these activities with accurate demand forecasts, businesses can create a more synchronized and responsive supply chain. The planning process ensures that all stakeholders—sales, marketing, production, procurement, and logistics—are on the same page when it comes to expected demand and supply availability.

The role of demand planning is not just about forecasting numbers; it is about creating a strategic approach to managing those numbers. A robust demand planning process ensures that the supply chain functions cohesively, minimizing inefficiencies while enhancing responsiveness to customer needs. When demand planning is done effectively, companies can maximize the profitability of their supply chain by striking the right balance between cost management and customer satisfaction.

Key Functions of Demand Planning

Demand planning involves several key functions that ensure alignment with organizational goals and market dynamics. These functions are intertwined with both internal and external processes, from sales and marketing to procurement and logistics.

Forecasting Demand

The foundation of demand planning is demand forecasting, which is the process of predicting future customer demand for products or services. Forecasting can be done using quantitative methods, such as historical sales data analysis, and qualitative methods, such as expert opinion or market research. Both methods have their strengths and are often combined to achieve more accurate predictions.

Quantitative forecasting methods, like time series analysis, regression analysis, and machine learning models, rely on historical data to project future demand patterns. These methods are particularly useful when there is a clear and consistent demand trend. However, demand can also be influenced by many external factors like seasonality, promotions, and economic changes, which require expert input and market insights for accurate forecasting.

Collaborative Demand Planning

Collaboration is an essential element of modern demand planning. In many organizations, demand planning is not the sole responsibility of one department. It requires close collaboration between sales, marketing, finance, and production teams. Sales teams can provide valuable insights into customer behavior and trends, marketing teams can share information on upcoming campaigns, and production teams can inform planners about any constraints or capacity limitations.

Collaborative planning helps align supply chain decisions with market realities. When all stakeholders are involved in the planning process, it leads to better communication, a shared understanding of goals, and improved decision-making. Collaborative demand planning can also help identify discrepancies between the forecasted demand and actual demand, enabling the company to take corrective actions quickly.

Inventory Management

Effective demand planning is closely linked to inventory management, which is a key part of maintaining balance in the supply chain. Inventory management ensures that the right amount of stock is available to meet customer demand without incurring excessive carrying costs. Through accurate demand forecasts, organizations can avoid both overstocking, which ties up valuable resources, and understocking, which can lead to missed sales and customer dissatisfaction.

Demand planners use forecasts to develop inventory policies that determine the optimal stock levels for various products. They take into account lead times, supplier performance, production capacity, and storage costs. The goal is to ensure that inventory is available when needed without overburdening the company with excess goods. Efficient inventory management, enabled by demand planning, reduces the risk of stockouts, backorders, and excess inventory, which can all lead to financial losses.

Production and Procurement Planning

Another critical function of demand planning is aligning production and procurement activities with the expected demand. Production planning ensures that manufacturing processes are optimized to meet forecasted demand without overproducing. Similarly, procurement planning ensures that the right materials and components are available when needed, in the right quantities, to support production schedules.

Effective demand planning enables companies to maintain the right balance in production, avoiding bottlenecks or excessive inventory buildup. It also provides procurement teams with accurate insights into the timing and quantity of required materials, allowing them to negotiate better contracts, reduce lead times, and optimize supplier relationships. This alignment reduces the risks of delays or disruptions in the supply chain.

Challenges in Demand Planning

While demand planning is essential to supply chain success, it is also fraught with challenges. These challenges are primarily due to the unpredictability of customer demand, external market factors, and operational constraints. Some common challenges in demand planning include:

Volatility in Demand

Customer demand can fluctuate unpredictably due to a variety of factors, including economic shifts, changes in consumer preferences, and unforeseen global events like natural disasters or pandemics. While historical data can provide a foundation for forecasting, demand planners must always be prepared for volatility. This requires flexibility and agility in the demand planning process, enabling companies to quickly adapt to unexpected changes.

Data Quality and Accuracy

The accuracy of demand forecasts depends heavily on the quality of the data used. Inaccurate, incomplete, or outdated data can lead to poor forecasting and supply chain inefficiencies. Organizations need to ensure that data is collected from reliable sources and that it is updated regularly. The use of data analytics tools can help in identifying trends and anomalies in the data, allowing for more accurate demand planning.

Siloed Operations

In many organizations, different departments (sales, marketing, production, and logistics) operate in silos, which can hinder the demand planning process. Without collaboration and communication across functions, demand planners may not have access to the most up-to-date market information, resulting in inaccurate forecasts and misaligned supply chain operations. Breaking down these silos and fostering cross-departmental collaboration is essential for effective demand planning.

Technological Integration

With the increasing complexity of supply chains, organizations need advanced technology solutions to support demand planning. Traditional spreadsheet-based forecasting models often fall short in handling large amounts of data and responding to dynamic market conditions. Advanced demand planning software, powered by artificial intelligence and machine learning, can enhance forecasting accuracy by analyzing vast amounts of data and predicting demand trends. However, integrating these technologies with existing supply chain systems can be challenging, requiring investment in both software and training.

Demand planning plays an integral role in the supply chain, serving as the bridge between customer demand and the operational capabilities of the organization. By accurately forecasting demand, organizations can optimize inventory levels, reduce costs, and improve customer satisfaction. The key to successful demand planning lies in collaboration, data accuracy, and technology integration, as well as the ability to adapt to changing market conditions. In a world of rapidly evolving customer expectations and global supply chain complexities, effective demand planning is no longer optional; it is a critical capability that organizations must master to stay competitive.

Forecasting Methods: Quantitative and Qualitative Approaches

Forecasting is a critical component of demand planning and supply chain management. It helps organizations predict future demand for products and services, allowing them to optimize inventory, production, and procurement processes. The ability to make accurate forecasts is vital for improving efficiency, minimizing costs, and ensuring customer satisfaction. There are two primary categories of forecasting methods: quantitative and qualitative. Both methods offer distinct advantages and are applied in different scenarios depending on the available data, business context, and the nature of the product or service being forecasted.

Quantitative Forecasting Methods

Quantitative forecasting methods are based on historical data and statistical models to predict future demand. These methods rely on the premise that past patterns, such as sales trends and market conditions, are indicative of future behavior. Quantitative forecasting is particularly useful when there is enough historical data to identify trends, patterns, and relationships. The main types of quantitative forecasting methods include time series analysis, causal models, and machine learning techniques.

Time Series Analysis

Time series analysis is one of the most widely used quantitative forecasting methods. It involves analyzing historical data points collected at regular intervals (e.g., daily, weekly, or monthly) to identify trends, cycles, and seasonality in the data. Time series forecasting assumes that past demand data will repeat in a similar pattern in the future, making it highly suitable for businesses with stable demand patterns.

The main components of time series analysis include:

Trend: The long-term movement in data, either increasing or decreasing over time.

Seasonality: The regular, predictable fluctuations that occur within specific periods, such as seasonal demand for winter clothes or holiday shopping.

Cyclic Patterns: The irregular, long-term fluctuations in data, typically driven by economic or business cycles.

Randomness: The unpredictable, random fluctuations that are not part of any trend or seasonality.

Common time series models used for forecasting include:

Moving Average: A simple method that calculates the average of a specified number of past periods. It smooths out short-term fluctuations and identifies longer-term trends.

Exponential Smoothing: A more advanced technique that gives more weight to recent data while still considering historical data. It can be adjusted to account for trends and seasonality.

Autoregressive Integrated Moving Average (ARIMA): A sophisticated time series model that combines autoregressive (AR) and moving average (MA) components to predict future values based on the relationship between past data points.

Causal Models

Causal forecasting methods involve using independent variables (predictors or drivers) that are believed to influence the demand for a product or service. These variables can include factors such as advertising spend, economic conditions, or competitor activity. Causal models are particularly useful when there are clear, identifiable relationships between the forecasted demand and influencing factors.

One common type of causal model is **regression analysis**, which establishes a mathematical relationship between a dependent variable (demand) and one or more independent variables (drivers). For example, a company may use regression analysis to forecast demand for a product based on the amount spent on marketing or the pricing strategy.

Machine Learning Techniques

Machine learning (ML) techniques have emerged as powerful tools for demand forecasting. These techniques can process large volumes of data and learn complex patterns in the data that traditional statistical methods may not capture. ML methods are particularly useful in environments with highly dynamic demand patterns or when there is a vast amount of data available from various sources.

Some popular machine learning algorithms used for forecasting include:

> **Decision Trees**: These models use a tree-like structure to break down complex decision-making processes, making them useful for predicting demand based on multiple factors.

> **Neural Networks**: A more advanced method inspired by the human brain's neural structure, neural networks can recognize patterns in data, making them useful for forecasting demand in highly non-linear systems.

Random Forest: A technique that builds multiple decision trees and combines their outputs to make more accurate predictions, often used when there are large datasets with many variables.

Machine learning-based forecasting methods offer improved accuracy over traditional methods, especially in industries where demand is highly volatile or influenced by many variables.

Qualitative Forecasting Methods

Qualitative forecasting methods rely on subjective judgment, intuition, and expert opinions rather than numerical data. These methods are typically used when historical data is unavailable, unreliable, or insufficient to make quantitative predictions. Qualitative forecasting is also helpful in predicting new product launches, market shifts, or changes in consumer behavior where quantitative data might not yet exist.

Some common qualitative forecasting methods include:

Expert Opinion (Delphi Method)

The Delphi Method is a structured approach that involves gathering insights from a panel of experts. The experts provide their opinions on future demand based on their knowledge, experience, and understanding of the market. The process typically involves multiple rounds of feedback, where experts review and refine their predictions in light of new information or insights from other panel members.

This method is often used when dealing with uncertain or rapidly changing markets, such as emerging technologies or products with limited historical data. The Delphi Method helps organizations tap into the collective wisdom of industry experts and make more informed predictions.

Market Research and Focus Groups

Market research involves collecting qualitative data directly from customers or potential customers to assess their preferences, purchasing intentions, and expectations. Surveys, focus groups, and interviews are common tools used in market research to gather insights into consumer behavior and demand trends.

Focus groups are particularly valuable for understanding customer attitudes toward a product, brand, or market trend. In a focus group, a moderator leads a discussion with a small group of individuals who represent the target market. The qualitative insights gathered during these sessions can help businesses gauge future demand, especially for new products or services.

Market research can also include competitor analysis, studying industry trends, and tracking economic indicators that may influence customer purchasing decisions. While market research does not provide hard numbers like quantitative forecasting, it can provide valuable directional insights into demand patterns.

Judgmental Forecasting

Judgmental forecasting involves relying on the subjective judgment of experienced managers, salespeople, or industry experts to make demand predictions. This approach is often used when data is sparse, or when there are external factors (e.g., political, economic, or social changes) that cannot be easily modeled using quantitative methods.

While judgmental forecasting can be useful in uncertain environments, it is highly dependent on the expertise and experience of the individuals involved. Biases or personal preferences can affect the accuracy of the forecast. Therefore, it is important to use judgmental forecasting in conjunction with other methods when possible, and to continually refine the process based on new data and insights.

Sales Force Composite

In the sales force composite method, salespeople are asked to estimate future sales based on their interactions with customers and their knowledge of market conditions. Salespeople often have a close relationship with customers and are in the best position to assess future demand based on customer inquiries, buying patterns, and feedback.

Sales force composite forecasting can be particularly effective for products with fluctuating demand or when market conditions change frequently. However, like judgmental forecasting, it can be influenced by personal biases and may require validation through other forecasting methods.

Choosing the Right Forecasting Method

The choice between quantitative and qualitative forecasting methods depends on several factors, including the availability of data, the complexity of the market, the forecast horizon, and the specific industry requirements. For example, quantitative methods like time series analysis are typically more accurate in stable markets with consistent demand patterns, while qualitative methods such as the Delphi Method are better suited for forecasting in uncertain or emerging markets where data is limited or unreliable.

In practice, many organizations use a combination of both approaches, often referred to as **hybrid forecasting**. By integrating both quantitative and qualitative methods, businesses can leverage the strengths of each and improve the accuracy and reliability of their forecasts. This hybrid approach is especially beneficial in dynamic environments where both historical data and expert judgment are essential to understanding future demand.

Forecasting methods, whether quantitative or qualitative, are essential tools for effective demand planning and supply chain management. Quantitative methods provide the foundation for data-driven decision-making, offering statistical models and algorithms to predict future demand based on historical trends. On the other hand, qualitative methods rely on expert judgment, market insights, and customer feedback to assess demand in uncertain or data-sparse environments. By understanding the strengths and limitations of each method and using them appropriately, organizations can improve the accuracy of their forecasts, optimize supply chain operations, and enhance customer satisfaction.

Collaborative Forecasting Techniques

In today's interconnected business environment, forecasting is no longer a solitary activity limited to internal teams; instead, it has evolved into a more collaborative process involving multiple stakeholders across the supply chain. Collaborative forecasting is a technique that integrates inputs from various partners, including suppliers, distributors, and even customers, to improve the accuracy and reliability of demand forecasts. This approach acknowledges that no single entity holds all the information required to make accurate predictions about demand, and by combining different perspectives, organizations can make more informed and precise forecasts.

Collaborative forecasting not only helps in improving the accuracy of demand predictions but also strengthens relationships among supply chain partners, promotes better decision-making, and enables the alignment of supply and demand across the entire value chain. By sharing relevant data, such as sales trends, inventory levels, and upcoming promotions, all stakeholders can work together to anticipate future demand more effectively.

Benefits of Collaborative Forecasting

Collaborative forecasting offers numerous advantages to both suppliers and buyers. By working together to create more accurate forecasts, organizations can enhance their operations in several key ways:

Improved Forecast Accuracy

By combining data and insights from multiple stakeholders, collaborative forecasting provides a more comprehensive view of demand trends. Suppliers and customers may have unique knowledge or visibility into aspects of demand that others do not. For instance, suppliers may know about potential disruptions in their production schedules, while customers might have insights into upcoming marketing campaigns or consumer behavior shifts. Sharing this information improves the overall forecast accuracy.

Enhanced Inventory Management

Collaborative forecasting reduces the likelihood of inventory stockouts or overstock situations. When suppliers, manufacturers, and retailers align their forecasts, they can better synchronize their production and ordering cycles, ensuring the right amount of inventory is available when it's needed. This minimizes holding costs while preventing the risk of lost sales due to stockouts.

Stronger Supplier and Customer Relationships

Working together to create accurate forecasts builds trust and strengthens relationships between partners. A collaborative approach fosters an environment of shared responsibility, where all parties are invested in the success of the entire supply chain rather than focusing solely on their individual interests. This leads to better communication, transparency, and mutual support among partners.

Optimized Production and Distribution Planning

With more accurate forecasts, production schedules and distribution plans can be better optimized. Manufacturers can plan their production runs to align with the forecasted demand, while distributors and retailers can adjust their replenishment strategies accordingly. This helps in improving operational efficiency, reducing lead times, and minimizing waste.

Better Decision-Making and Risk Mitigation

Collaboration provides access to a wider range of insights, allowing for better-informed decisions. By sharing information about potential risks, such as raw material shortages, economic shifts, or unexpected demand spikes, supply chain partners can jointly develop risk mitigation strategies. This can help in avoiding disruptions and maintaining smooth operations even in uncertain environments.

Collaborative Forecasting Techniques

There are several techniques and frameworks through which organizations can engage in collaborative forecasting. These techniques involve varying levels of communication, data sharing, and coordination among supply chain partners. The most common collaborative forecasting techniques include:

Sales and Operations Planning (S&OP)

Sales and Operations Planning (S&OP) is one of the most popular collaborative forecasting methods. S&OP is a process that aligns the sales, marketing, and operations teams within an organization to ensure that demand forecasts align with supply capabilities. The S&OP process typically includes the following steps:

Data Gathering: Sales and marketing teams gather data on historical sales, market trends, and upcoming promotions.

Demand Forecasting: The demand planning team uses this data to create forecasts for future demand, adjusting for seasonality, trends, and external factors.

Supply Planning: The supply chain team reviews the forecast and plans production, procurement, and inventory strategies to meet the forecasted demand.

Balancing Supply and Demand: The teams collaborate to identify any gaps between supply and demand and work to address those gaps by adjusting inventory levels, production schedules, or sales strategies.

The key to successful S&OP is cross-functional collaboration. Sales, marketing, operations, and finance teams must collaborate closely to ensure that the forecast reflects both market conditions and operational capabilities. Involving external partners, such as suppliers, in the process further improves forecast accuracy by incorporating their insights into production capacity and lead times.

Collaborative Planning, Forecasting, and Replenishment (CPFR)

Collaborative Planning, Forecasting, and Replenishment (CPFR) is an advanced collaborative forecasting technique that extends beyond internal teams to include supply chain partners, such as suppliers, distributors, and customers. CPFR aims to synchronize supply chain activities and streamline the flow of goods by creating a shared forecast and aligning all partners on production and replenishment plans.

The CPFR process involves the following steps:

Strategy and Planning: Partners agree on objectives and key performance indicators (KPIs) for the collaboration.

Demand Forecasting: Partners share historical sales data and other relevant information to jointly create a demand forecast.

Replenishment Planning: Based on the forecast, partners align their replenishment strategies, determining when and how much product to order or produce.

Execution: Suppliers and retailers execute the replenishment plans, ensuring that inventory levels are maintained and stockouts are minimized.

Performance Monitoring: Partners continuously monitor performance against the forecast, adjusting as necessary to account for changes in demand or supply conditions.

CPFR is highly beneficial for industries with complex supply chains or products with fluctuating demand patterns. It helps in reducing the bullwhip effect, where small fluctuations in demand lead to larger fluctuations in supply chain activities, resulting in inefficiencies and increased costs.

Vendor-Managed Inventory (VMI)

Vendor-Managed Inventory (VMI) is a collaborative approach in which the supplier is responsible for managing the inventory levels at the customer's location. In this arrangement, the supplier has access to real-time data on inventory levels and sales at the customer's site, allowing them to make more accurate decisions about when to replenish stock.

VMI reduces the risk of stockouts, as suppliers are better equipped to monitor demand fluctuations and adjust inventory levels accordingly. By working together in this way, both the supplier and the customer share the responsibility for maintaining optimal inventory levels. This leads to more efficient inventory management and reduced costs associated with stockouts and overstocking.

Demand Signal Repository (DSR)

A Demand Signal Repository (DSR) is a centralized system that aggregates data from various sources within the supply chain, including point-of-sale (POS) systems, inventory management systems, and external market data. The DSR collects and stores real-time data on product demand, enabling supply chain partners to make more informed decisions.

The DSR serves as a central repository where data can be accessed by both suppliers and customers. By integrating data from multiple sources, it ensures that all parties are working with the same set of information when creating demand forecasts. This reduces discrepancies in forecasting and helps supply chain partners stay aligned in their efforts to meet customer demand.

Collaborative Demand Sensing

Demand sensing refers to the process of using real-time data and advanced analytics to detect changes in demand patterns more quickly. Collaborative demand sensing involves working with external partners, such as suppliers and retailers, to share real-time data on sales, promotions, and inventory levels. This allows organizations to adjust their demand forecasts and supply plans more dynamically in response to changing conditions.

For example, if a retailer experiences a sudden surge in demand for a particular product due to a promotional campaign, sharing that information with suppliers in real-time enables them to adjust production or procurement plans accordingly. This reduces the risk of stockouts and ensures that customers' needs are met without excessive inventory buildup.

Challenges in Collaborative Forecasting

While collaborative forecasting offers significant benefits, it is not without its challenges. Some common obstacles to successful collaboration include:

Data Sharing Issues: Organizations may be reluctant to share sensitive data, such as sales figures or inventory levels, due to concerns about confidentiality or competitive advantage.

Lack of Trust: Collaborative forecasting requires a high level of trust among supply chain partners. Without trust, partners may be hesitant to share accurate data or may act in ways that are counterproductive to the overall goals of the collaboration.

Coordination Complexity: Coordinating across multiple stakeholders can be complex, especially when dealing with large, global supply chains. Different partners may have different systems, processes, and priorities, making it difficult to align efforts.

Data Quality: The accuracy and timeliness of the data used in collaborative forecasting are critical. Poor-quality data can lead to inaccurate forecasts, undermining the effectiveness of the collaboration.

Conclusion

Collaborative forecasting is a vital tool in today's complex supply chains, offering numerous benefits in terms of improving forecast accuracy, reducing costs, optimizing inventory, and enhancing relationships between partners. By combining the strengths of quantitative and qualitative forecasting techniques with collaborative efforts across stakeholders, organizations can achieve more accurate demand predictions and better align their supply chain activities with actual demand. However, successful implementation requires overcoming challenges related to data sharing, trust, and coordination. When executed well, collaborative forecasting can lead to significant improvements in supply chain efficiency, ultimately benefiting all partners involved.

Chapter 9: Inventory Management and Optimization

Types of Inventory and Their Roles

Effective inventory management is critical for businesses seeking to maintain a balance between supply and demand, optimize operational efficiency, and reduce costs. Inventory management involves controlling and overseeing the stored goods that a company uses in its operations. Different types of inventory serve distinct roles within the supply chain, each playing a vital part in meeting customer demand while ensuring the smooth flow of materials, products, and services.

Inventory is categorized into different types based on its function in the production process or sales cycle. Understanding these types, their roles, and their interaction with one another allows businesses to make informed decisions on procurement, storage, and distribution. The primary types of inventory include raw materials, work-in-progress (WIP), finished goods, maintenance, repair, and operating supplies (MRO), and transit inventory.

Raw Materials Inventory

Raw materials are the foundational inputs used in manufacturing and production processes. These materials are sourced from suppliers and serve as the base for creating finished products. Raw materials inventory is the first stage of inventory in the production process, and it consists of unprocessed goods that have yet to be transformed into the final product.

Role of Raw Materials: The role of raw materials is critical to the functioning of the production process. Without sufficient raw materials, production can be delayed or halted, which can negatively affect a company's ability to meet customer demand and its bottom line. Proper management of raw materials is vital to ensure that businesses avoid overstocking, which can lead to increased storage costs, or understocking, which can cause production bottlenecks. Raw materials are managed carefully through techniques like Economic Order Quantity (EOQ) to ensure optimal inventory levels.

Work-in-Progress (WIP) Inventory

Work-in-progress inventory consists of items that are in the process of being transformed into finished products but have not yet completed the manufacturing cycle. WIP inventory represents materials that have been partially processed, and it includes products that are at different stages of production.

Role of WIP: The role of WIP inventory is to maintain a steady flow of production between the raw material stage and the finished goods stage. Having an adequate WIP inventory allows manufacturers to avoid delays in the production process and ensures that there is always a stock of partially completed goods ready to move to the next phase of manufacturing. WIP inventory also helps in smoothing production flow, particularly when there are variations in lead times or supply chain disruptions. However, businesses must carefully manage WIP inventory to avoid overproduction, as excess WIP ties up capital and storage space.

Finished Goods Inventory

Finished goods inventory consists of products that have completed the entire production process and are ready for sale or distribution. These goods are the final output of manufacturing or assembly operations and are typically stored in warehouses until they are sold or shipped to customers.

Role of Finished Goods: Finished goods are the most important inventory type for customer satisfaction and sales revenue. The role of finished goods is to ensure that customer demand can be met promptly. A business must balance the amount of finished goods it holds to avoid stockouts (which can lead to lost sales and customer dissatisfaction) and overstocking (which can incur storage costs and the risk of obsolete goods). Finished goods inventory is often managed using demand forecasting techniques, and it plays a critical role in maintaining service levels and optimizing order fulfillment processes. Efficient finished goods inventory management ensures that products are readily available to customers without tying up excess capital in unsold goods.

Maintenance, Repair, and Operating (MRO) Supplies

MRO supplies are the materials and equipment used in the maintenance, repair, and operation of machinery, production equipment, and other assets necessary for business operations. These supplies are often overlooked compared to raw materials and finished goods but are nonetheless vital to the ongoing functioning of production and other operational activities.

Role of MRO: MRO supplies play an essential role in ensuring that machinery and equipment remain functional. Regular maintenance and timely repairs prevent costly breakdowns that could halt production, leading to significant delays and lost revenue. MRO inventory includes items such as tools, lubricants, safety equipment, and spare parts. Proper MRO inventory management ensures that the necessary supplies are available when needed while minimizing excess inventory and associated costs. Without effective management of MRO supplies, businesses risk extended downtime and increased operational disruptions.

Transit Inventory

Transit inventory refers to goods that are in the process of being transported between locations, whether it is from a supplier to a manufacturer, from a manufacturer to a distributor, or from a distributor to a retailer. Transit inventory is the goods that are physically on their way through the supply chain but have not yet reached their final destination.

Role of Transit Inventory: The role of transit inventory is to account for the time goods spend in transit and ensure that they are available for use or sale when they arrive at the next location in the supply chain. Transit inventory can affect overall lead times, as it takes into account transportation durations, customs delays, and other logistical issues. Efficient management of transit inventory is crucial for reducing lead times and ensuring timely deliveries. Companies that track their transit inventory accurately can better anticipate supply chain delays and adjust their internal processes, such as production or sales, to compensate for any disruptions.

Cycle Inventory

Cycle inventory refers to the inventory that is regularly replenished through a continuous ordering process. This inventory type is used to meet expected demand during a specific period, such as weekly, monthly, or quarterly. It is commonly seen in businesses that sell products with stable demand patterns, where goods are ordered in bulk and consumed gradually over time.

Role of Cycle Inventory: Cycle inventory plays a central role in managing day-to-day operations. The primary function of cycle inventory is to ensure that businesses have enough stock to meet routine customer demand without overstocking. It is the inventory held between order cycles, so it needs to be replenished regularly based on demand forecasts. Proper cycle inventory management reduces the risks associated with stockouts and overstocking while enabling businesses to operate efficiently within the constraints of their purchasing and ordering systems.

Safety Stock

Safety stock is extra inventory that a business holds in reserve to protect against uncertainty in demand or supply. This inventory is not part of regular cycle inventory but is maintained as a buffer to cover unexpected spikes in demand or delays in supply.

Role of Safety Stock: The role of safety stock is to act as a safeguard against uncertainties in the supply chain. Variations in customer demand, lead time variability, and supply chain disruptions can result in stockouts, which can negatively impact customer satisfaction and sales. Safety stock ensures that businesses can continue to meet customer demand even in the face of unforeseen fluctuations. The key to effective safety stock management is to calculate an optimal level of safety inventory, balancing the risk of stockouts with the costs of holding excess inventory.

Decoupling Inventory

Decoupling inventory refers to inventory held between two production or supply chain stages to buffer against potential disruptions in one stage. For example, a company may keep a stock of finished sub-assemblies between different stages of assembly to ensure that if one stage experiences a delay, the next stage can continue uninterrupted.

Role of Decoupling Inventory: The role of decoupling inventory is to smooth production and ensure continuity in the event of disruptions. This inventory type helps prevent delays and keeps production lines operating even if one part of the supply chain experiences a delay. While decoupling inventory helps minimize production stoppages, it must be managed carefully to avoid excessive buildup, which can lead to higher storage costs and obsolescence risks.

Role of Inventory in Supply Chain Management

Each type of inventory plays a crucial role in the broader context of supply chain management. Properly managing different types of inventory allows businesses to balance production schedules, sales goals, and customer expectations. Inventory also serves as a buffer against demand fluctuations, supply chain disruptions, and other uncertainties that can affect a company's ability to meet its objectives.

The ultimate goal of inventory management is to ensure that businesses have the right amount of inventory at the right time, minimizing costs and maximizing operational efficiency. Advanced techniques, such as

Just-in-Time (JIT), Economic Order Quantity (EOQ), and demand forecasting, can help optimize inventory levels and ensure that supply chains function smoothly and effectively.

Inventory is the lifeblood of supply chain operations, and understanding the roles of different types of inventory is critical to managing it effectively. Raw materials, WIP, finished goods, MRO supplies, transit inventory, cycle inventory, safety stock, and decoupling inventory all contribute to different aspects of the production, distribution, and sales processes. By optimizing inventory levels and managing each type strategically, businesses can reduce operational costs, improve customer satisfaction, and enhance overall supply chain performance. Inventory management is not a one-size-fits-all approach; it requires careful planning, analysis, and continuous improvement to meet the dynamic demands of modern supply chains.

Techniques for Inventory Control (EOQ, Safety Stock)

Effective inventory control is essential for businesses to meet customer demand while minimizing costs. Proper inventory management allows organizations to maintain an optimal balance between stock availability and storage expenses. Among the most widely used techniques for inventory control are **Economic Order Quantity (EOQ)** and **Safety Stock**. Both of these methods serve distinct but complementary roles in inventory management, ensuring that businesses can operate efficiently and effectively.

In this section, we explore these two techniques in detail, examining their principles, applications, and how they contribute to the overall efficiency of supply chain and inventory management systems.

Economic Order Quantity (EOQ)

The Economic Order Quantity (EOQ) model is one of the oldest and most fundamental techniques used in inventory control. It is a formula used by businesses to determine the optimal order quantity that minimizes the total cost of inventory. The goal of EOQ is to find the balance between two key inventory costs: **ordering costs** and **holding costs**.

Ordering Costs refer to the costs associated with placing and receiving orders, including administrative expenses, transportation fees, and any other costs incurred in the purchasing process. On the other hand, **Holding Costs** (also known as carrying costs) include expenses related to storing inventory, such as warehousing, insurance, and depreciation.

The EOQ formula is:

$$EOQ = \sqrt{\frac{2DS}{H}}$$

Where:

D = Demand for the product (usually annual demand)

S = Ordering cost per order

H = Holding cost per unit per year

Principles of EOQ

EOQ assumes a steady demand for inventory, consistent lead times, and the absence of quantity discounts. By calculating the EOQ, businesses can identify the most cost-effective order size that minimizes both ordering and holding costs.

Ordering Costs: When a company places frequent orders, the ordering costs increase, as each order incurs additional administrative costs. However, the company benefits from lower holding costs, as it keeps less inventory on hand.

Holding Costs: If a company orders large quantities less frequently, its holding costs increase, since it needs more space to store inventory. However, it reduces ordering costs by placing fewer orders.

EOQ seeks to balance these two opposing forces. By determining the optimal order quantity, companies can minimize the total cost of inventory, which is crucial for achieving efficiency in the supply chain.

Applications of EOQ

EOQ is most effective for products with steady and predictable demand, and when the cost of placing an order and holding inventory is relatively stable. It is commonly used in businesses with relatively simple, consistent inventory needs, such as manufacturing firms and retail stores with well-established product lines.

While EOQ provides a mathematical approach to inventory management, it is important to note that it assumes certain conditions, such as constant demand and lead times. In real-world situations, these conditions may fluctuate, requiring adjustments to the EOQ model. Businesses can address this by integrating dynamic forecasting techniques and periodic inventory reviews to adapt to changing conditions.

Safety Stock

Safety Stock refers to the extra inventory kept on hand to guard against uncertainties in demand and supply. It acts as a buffer against the unpredictability of both supply chain disruptions and fluctuations in customer demand. By maintaining safety stock, businesses can avoid stockouts—situations where inventory levels are too low to meet customer demand, which could result in lost sales and diminished customer satisfaction.

Principles of Safety Stock

The primary purpose of safety stock is to mitigate the risk of stockouts due to variations in demand or delays in supply chain processes. It is particularly useful in situations where demand is unpredictable or lead times from suppliers are uncertain.

The amount of safety stock to maintain is typically determined by factors such as:

Demand Variability: If demand for a product is highly variable, it is essential to carry a larger safety stock to cover unexpected surges in customer orders.

Lead Time Variability: If the lead time for replenishing inventory fluctuates, higher safety stock may be required to buffer against delays in receiving stock from suppliers.

Service Level: Businesses often determine the level of service they wish to provide customers. A higher service level means fewer stockouts and greater customer satisfaction, but it may require larger safety stocks.

Applications of Safety Stock

Safety stock is applied to prevent stockouts caused by unpredictable changes in demand or delays in supply. It is most commonly used in industries where demand fluctuates frequently, or where lead times from suppliers are long or inconsistent. For example, retail businesses that sell seasonal products, or manufacturers that rely on suppliers with varying delivery times, use safety stock to reduce the risk of running out of stock during peak demand periods.

Calculating the correct amount of safety stock can be complex, as it involves estimating demand and lead time variations. Overestimating safety stock can lead to higher holding costs, while underestimating it can result in stockouts. Businesses can fine-tune safety stock levels by regularly reviewing sales data, supply chain performance, and changes in customer demand patterns.

Determining the Optimal Level of Safety Stock

The optimal level of safety stock balances the cost of holding excess inventory with the risk of stockouts. It is essential for businesses to consider factors like lead time variability and demand fluctuations when calculating the appropriate amount of safety stock. Too little safety stock could result in lost sales and missed opportunities, while too much could tie up capital in unnecessary inventory and increase holding costs.

Some businesses use advanced inventory management systems to help monitor demand variability and lead time performance. These systems allow businesses to adjust safety stock levels dynamically in response to changing conditions.

Integration of EOQ and Safety Stock in Inventory Management

While EOQ and safety stock are distinct inventory control techniques, they can complement each other when used in tandem. EOQ helps businesses determine the optimal order quantity that minimizes the combined costs of ordering and holding inventory, while safety stock serves as a buffer against uncertainties that may disrupt the supply chain.

Incorporating both techniques allows businesses to operate efficiently while ensuring they have adequate inventory levels to meet customer demand. For example, when calculating EOQ, companies can include safety stock as part of the total inventory needs. The result is a more comprehensive inventory strategy that minimizes costs and ensures high levels of customer satisfaction.

Moreover, in industries with highly volatile demand or unreliable supply chains, businesses might prioritize safety stock over minimizing holding costs, ensuring that they can fulfill orders even during periods of unexpected demand spikes or delays in the supply chain.

Both **Economic Order Quantity (EOQ)** and **Safety Stock** are essential techniques in inventory control that help businesses optimize their inventory levels. EOQ focuses on minimizing the total cost of inventory by determining the most cost-effective order quantity, while safety stock helps mitigate the risks of stockouts by providing a buffer for unexpected demand or supply fluctuations. By integrating these two techniques, businesses can achieve a balanced and effective inventory control system, ensuring that they can meet customer demand while managing costs efficiently. Advanced inventory management systems and regular monitoring of demand and supply conditions are critical to maintaining optimal inventory levels and adapting to the dynamic needs of modern supply chains.

Inventory Optimization in Supply Chains

Inventory optimization is a critical function in supply chain management, aiming to ensure that an organization maintains the right level of inventory to meet customer demand while minimizing costs. It involves balancing inventory availability with holding costs, ensuring efficient use of working capital, and reducing risks such as stockouts or excess inventory. Proper inventory optimization can significantly improve a company's operational efficiency, enhance customer satisfaction, and contribute to overall business profitability.

In modern supply chains, inventory optimization goes beyond just managing stock levels. It involves strategic decision-making, leveraging technology, and employing advanced methodologies to optimize inventory performance. This chapter explores the concept of inventory optimization, its importance in supply chains, the various methods and strategies employed, and the role of technology in achieving optimization goals.

Importance of Inventory Optimization in Supply Chains

Efficient inventory management is a cornerstone of any well-functioning supply chain. Inventory represents a significant portion of working capital, and ineffective management of it can lead to increased costs, such as storage, handling, and stock obsolescence. On the other hand, holding too little inventory can lead to stockouts, which can cause customer dissatisfaction and lost sales opportunities.

Inventory optimization focuses on finding the delicate balance between having enough inventory to fulfill customer demand without overstocking, which ties up capital. The benefits of optimizing inventory include:

> **Cost Reduction:** By optimizing inventory levels, companies can minimize holding and storage costs, as well as reduce the risk of obsolete stock.
>
> **Improved Cash Flow:** Reducing excess inventory frees up capital that can be used for other strategic investments, thereby improving the company's liquidity and cash flow.
>
> **Customer Satisfaction:** Inventory optimization ensures that products are available when customers need them, thereby preventing stockouts and backorders, and improving on-time delivery rates.
>
> **Supply Chain Efficiency:** Streamlining inventory levels reduces the complexity of supply chain processes, leading to more efficient warehousing, transportation, and order fulfillment.

Key Components of Inventory Optimization

Inventory optimization typically involves several components, each of which contributes to achieving a balance between customer demand and cost control. These components include:

> **Demand Forecasting:** Accurate demand forecasting is essential for inventory optimization. By predicting future demand based on historical data, market trends, and customer behavior, businesses can determine the right levels of inventory

needed to meet that demand. Techniques like moving averages, exponential smoothing, and more advanced machine learning methods can help improve forecasting accuracy.

Replenishment Strategies: Replenishment strategies are designed to determine when and how much inventory to order to avoid stockouts while minimizing excess stock. Common strategies include the **Just-in-Time (JIT)** method, which aims to receive inventory only when it's needed, and the **Economic Order Quantity (EOQ)** model, which calculates the optimal order quantity to minimize ordering and holding costs.

Lead Time Management: Lead time, or the time it takes for an order to be delivered from the supplier to the warehouse, significantly affects inventory optimization. Reducing lead times can help improve inventory flow and minimize the need for safety stock. Proper coordination with suppliers and logistics providers is essential to minimize delays and ensure inventory is replenished in a timely manner.

Safety Stock Management: Safety stock acts as a buffer to protect against unexpected demand surges or supply chain disruptions. While safety stock is an important tool in preventing stockouts, excessive safety stock leads to increased holding costs. Optimizing safety stock involves finding the right amount of buffer inventory to manage demand fluctuations and supply delays.

Inventory Segmentation: Not all inventory is created equal. High-demand products should be prioritized in inventory management, while slow-moving or obsolete items should be minimized or eliminated. Segmentation techniques such as **ABC Analysis** categorize inventory based on criteria like sales volume, demand variability, and value, enabling businesses to allocate resources and management efforts accordingly.

Inventory Optimization Strategies

Several strategies can be employed to optimize inventory within a supply chain. These strategies aim to balance customer demand, stock levels, and costs, while improving overall supply chain performance. Some of the most commonly used strategies include:

Just-in-Time (JIT): The JIT strategy focuses on reducing inventory levels by ordering goods only when they are needed, rather than holding large amounts of stock. By synchronizing production and inventory with actual demand, JIT minimizes storage costs and reduces the risk of overstocking. However, JIT requires a highly responsive supply chain with minimal lead times and reliable suppliers to avoid stockouts.

Vendor-Managed Inventory (VMI): Under a VMI model, the supplier manages the inventory levels of the customer, ensuring that the right products are delivered at the right time. This approach helps optimize inventory levels by leveraging supplier expertise and data, enabling faster restocking and reducing the burden of inventory management on the buyer.

Drop Shipping: Drop shipping is a fulfillment method where the retailer doesn't maintain inventory in-house but instead transfers customer orders directly to a manufacturer or wholesaler, who then ships the goods directly to the customer. This approach eliminates the need for inventory storage and handling, although it requires effective supplier coordination and communication.

Inventory Turnover Optimization: Inventory turnover refers to how frequently inventory is sold and replaced within a given period. High turnover rates indicate that inventory is being sold quickly, which is generally a sign of efficient inventory management. However, too high a turnover rate may lead to stockouts, while low turnover may indicate overstocking or poor sales performance. Optimizing inventory turnover involves finding the right balance to maintain product availability without overcommitting capital.

Collaborative Planning, Forecasting, and Replenishment (CPFR): CPFR is a strategy that involves collaboration between suppliers, manufacturers, and retailers to improve the accuracy of demand forecasts and inventory replenishment. By sharing data on inventory levels, demand patterns, and sales forecasts, all parties can work together to optimize stock levels and minimize excess inventory.

Role of Technology in Inventory Optimization

Technology plays an increasingly important role in inventory optimization, enabling businesses to manage inventory more effectively, automate key processes, and gain deeper insights into supply chain dynamics. Some of the key technological solutions that facilitate inventory optimization include:

Inventory Management Software: Modern inventory management systems provide real-time visibility into inventory levels, sales trends, and supply chain performance. These systems often come with advanced forecasting capabilities, automated reorder points, and integration with other enterprise resource planning (ERP) systems to streamline operations.

Advanced Analytics and Machine Learning: By leveraging historical data, machine learning algorithms can identify patterns in demand, supply chain disruptions, and other factors affecting inventory levels. These insights allow companies to fine-tune their inventory strategies and make more informed decisions regarding ordering, replenishment, and safety stock levels.

Radio Frequency Identification (RFID) and Internet of Things (IoT): RFID tags and IoT sensors enable businesses to track inventory in real time, improving accuracy and visibility.

These technologies can be used to monitor stock levels, track products throughout the supply chain, and ensure that inventory is stored in optimal conditions.

Blockchain Technology: Blockchain offers a transparent and secure way to manage supply chain data, including inventory levels and movements. It provides real-time tracking of goods, enhancing visibility and trust between suppliers, manufacturers, and distributors. Blockchain can also help improve traceability and reduce the risk of fraud and errors in the supply chain.

Challenges in Inventory Optimization

While inventory optimization offers significant benefits, achieving the right balance is often challenging. Some of the key challenges businesses face include:

Demand Volatility: Predicting customer demand is one of the most difficult aspects of inventory optimization. Fluctuations in customer behavior, seasonal variations, and market trends can make accurate forecasting difficult, leading to either overstocking or stockouts.

Supply Chain Disruptions: Disruptions in the supply chain, such as supplier delays, transportation issues, or geopolitical events, can complicate inventory management. Companies must be prepared to deal with these risks by implementing contingency plans and maintaining safety stock to buffer against these uncertainties.

Data Accuracy: Accurate and up-to-date data is essential for effective inventory optimization. Inaccurate or incomplete inventory records can lead to poor decision-making and inefficiencies, resulting in excess stock or stockouts.

Balancing Costs: Optimizing inventory involves balancing multiple costs, such as ordering, holding, and shortage costs. Finding the right mix of inventory strategies that minimizes costs while meeting customer demand can be a complex and ongoing process.

Inventory optimization is a dynamic and crucial aspect of supply chain management that involves finding the right balance between inventory availability and cost efficiency. By employing effective strategies such as **Just-in-Time (JIT)**, **Vendor-Managed Inventory (VMI)**, and **Collaborative Planning, Forecasting, and Replenishment (CPFR)**, businesses can reduce excess inventory, improve cash flow, and enhance customer satisfaction.

With the increasing reliance on technology, modern businesses can leverage advanced tools like **inventory management software**, **machine learning**, and **IoT** to optimize inventory more effectively. Despite the challenges of demand volatility, supply chain disruptions, and data accuracy, businesses that successfully optimize their inventory can achieve greater supply chain resilience, cost savings, and customer loyalty.

Chapter 10: Logistics and Distribution Management

Transportation Modes and Selection Criteria

Transportation is a critical element of logistics and distribution management, directly affecting the cost, speed, and reliability of the supply chain. Effective transportation management ensures the timely and cost-efficient movement of goods from suppliers to customers, contributing to the overall efficiency of a company's operations. The selection of the appropriate transportation mode is fundamental in achieving these objectives, as it involves a complex decision-making process that balances cost, delivery time, reliability, and flexibility.

This chapter focuses on the various transportation modes available in logistics and the criteria used to select the most suitable mode for specific supply chain needs. Understanding the strengths and weaknesses of each mode and applying the appropriate selection criteria are essential for optimizing transportation management.

Types of Transportation Modes

Transportation modes are classified based on the physical means used to move goods. Each mode has its unique advantages and limitations, making it suitable for different types of shipments, destinations, and business needs. The five primary modes of transportation are:

> **Road Transportation:** This is one of the most commonly used modes of transportation, especially for domestic shipments. It involves moving goods via trucks, lorries, or vans along roadways. Road transportation is highly flexible, offering door-to-door service, and it is suitable for a wide range of products, including those that need to be transported over short or medium distances. It is often used for shipments

within a country or region, and it can handle both small and large loads.

Advantages:

Flexibility and accessibility to remote locations

Relatively low cost for short distances

Quick transit times for local deliveries

Door-to-door delivery

Ability to handle a wide range of cargo types

Disadvantages:

Susceptible to road congestion, traffic delays, and adverse weather conditions

Limited by road infrastructure and distances

Regulatory restrictions such as weight limits and road usage permits

Rail Transportation: Rail transport is used for moving goods by train, typically over long distances within a country or across borders. This mode is well-suited for heavy, bulky items and large shipments that need to be transported in bulk, such as coal, agricultural products, and automotive parts. Rail transport is more energy-efficient than road transport and is ideal for shipments requiring relatively low transit times over longer distances.

Advantages:

Suitable for large-volume and bulk shipments

Lower environmental impact compared to road transportation

Cost-effective for long-distance transportation

More reliable in terms of on-time delivery, compared to road transport

Disadvantages:

Limited to rail networks and infrastructure

Lack of flexibility in terms of door-to-door delivery

Slower transit times compared to road or air transportation

Air Transportation: Air transport is the fastest mode of transportation, used primarily for high-value, time-sensitive, or perishable goods. It involves the movement of goods via cargo planes, either through scheduled airfreight services or chartered flights. Air transportation is ideal for shipments requiring urgent delivery, such as electronics, pharmaceuticals, and spare parts. Despite its higher cost, air transportation is often the preferred choice for global trade, especially for time-critical shipments.

Advantages:

Fastest mode of transport, ensuring rapid delivery

Suitable for high-value or perishable goods

Global reach, with the ability to serve international destinations

Higher reliability in terms of on-time delivery

Disadvantages:

High cost compared to other modes of transport

Limited cargo space and weight restrictions

Not suitable for large or bulky shipments

Dependent on airport infrastructure and regulations

Water Transportation: This mode involves moving goods via ships, vessels, and barges across oceans, rivers, and lakes. Water transport is used primarily for international trade and bulk commodities such as oil, grains, coal, and consumer goods. Water transportation is highly cost-effective for large-volume shipments and long distances, though it is relatively slow compared to other modes.

Advantages:

Very cost-effective for large-volume, bulk shipments

Ideal for international trade and long-distance transportation

Capable of carrying oversized and heavy cargo

Low environmental impact in terms of emissions, especially for bulk shipments

Disadvantages:

Slow transit times, often taking several days or weeks

Limited by port availability and infrastructure

Potential delays due to weather, tides, and port congestion

Vulnerable to geopolitical factors, piracy, and regulations

Pipeline Transportation: Pipelines are used primarily for transporting liquids and gases, such as oil, natural gas, and chemicals. This mode involves the movement of goods through a network of pipelines over long distances. While not suitable for general cargo, pipelines are essential for the energy sector, where large quantities of liquid or gaseous materials need to be transported safely and continuously.

Advantages:

Efficient and cost-effective for transporting liquids and gases

Reliable and continuous flow of goods

Minimal environmental impact once established

Reduced risks of delays or accidents compared to road or rail

Disadvantages:

Not suitable for solid or general cargo

High initial investment in infrastructure

Limited flexibility in terms of routing and delivery points

Criteria for Selecting the Appropriate Transportation Mode

Selecting the right transportation mode is critical for optimizing logistics costs, delivery performance, and overall supply chain efficiency. The decision to use one mode over another depends on several factors that can influence both operational and financial outcomes. Key criteria for selecting the most appropriate transportation mode include:

> **Cost:** One of the most important factors in mode selection is the total cost of transportation, which includes the direct costs such as freight charges, handling fees, and fuel costs, as well as indirect costs such as insurance, customs clearance, and port handling. Each mode has its cost structure, and businesses must assess which option provides the best balance between cost and service level. Road transportation is generally the least expensive for short distances, while air transportation tends to be the most costly.
>
> **Speed:** The urgency of the delivery is another crucial consideration when selecting a transportation mode. Air transport offers the fastest transit time, making it ideal for time-sensitive or perishable goods. On the other hand, rail and water transportation are slower, making them suitable for bulk or low-priority shipments that have longer delivery windows.
>
> **Reliability:** Reliability refers to the consistency and predictability of delivery times. Air transport is often the most reliable, with relatively few delays compared to other modes. Rail transportation is also known for its reliability, while road and water transportation are more susceptible to disruptions due to traffic, weather, and infrastructure limitations.
>
> **Cargo Type and Size:** The nature and characteristics of the cargo play a significant role in determining the appropriate mode of transportation. For example, oversized or heavy cargo

may require rail, water, or road transport, while high-value or delicate items may be better suited for air transport due to the increased security and speed. Perishable goods, such as fresh produce or pharmaceuticals, typically require air transport or refrigerated vehicles to maintain product integrity.

Distance: The distance the goods need to travel is a major determinant in transportation mode selection. For short distances, road transport is generally the most efficient option, while longer distances may be more cost-effective with rail, water, or air transportation, depending on the other factors involved.

Environmental Impact: With the increasing emphasis on sustainability, the environmental impact of transportation is becoming more important in mode selection. Water and rail transport are generally more environmentally friendly than road and air transport, due to lower emissions and more efficient fuel use. Companies committed to reducing their carbon footprint may prioritize these modes over others, depending on the shipment's requirements.

Infrastructure Availability: The availability of suitable infrastructure, such as roads, rail networks, ports, and airports, is a key consideration. Some regions may be better served by specific modes of transportation due to the presence of developed infrastructure. For instance, shipping is often the preferred mode for goods transported to and from regions with access to major ports, while landlocked areas may rely more heavily on road or rail transport.

Flexibility and Accessibility: Road transport is the most flexible mode of transportation, offering door-to-door service and access to remote areas. It is ideal for shipments that require last-mile delivery. In contrast, other modes such as rail or water transportation are less flexible and typically require additional handling and transfer at terminals or ports.

The selection of the appropriate transportation mode is a critical decision in logistics and distribution management. Each mode—road, rail, air, water, and pipeline—has its own advantages and limitations, making it suitable for different types of shipments and business requirements. The decision to use one mode over another depends on various factors, including cost, speed, reliability, cargo type, distance, and infrastructure availability.

By carefully evaluating these factors and considering the strategic goals of the business, supply chain professionals can optimize transportation decisions, reduce costs, improve service levels, and enhance the overall efficiency of the supply chain. Effective transportation management not only ensures timely and cost-effective delivery but also plays a vital role in achieving customer satisfaction and supporting business growth.

Warehousing and Distribution Strategies

In the modern supply chain, warehousing and distribution are pivotal components that play a significant role in ensuring the efficient and effective movement of goods from suppliers to customers. These two elements of logistics are closely intertwined, each influencing the other in terms of inventory management, cost, customer satisfaction, and overall supply chain performance. As global trade and consumer demand evolve, businesses are increasingly adopting sophisticated warehousing and distribution strategies to optimize operations and maintain competitiveness.

Warehousing refers to the storage of goods and materials for short-term or long-term use, typically in a warehouse or storage facility. Distribution involves the process of delivering those goods to the end consumer, whether that be a business, retailer, or individual customer. Both warehousing and distribution strategies need to be aligned with the overarching goals of the supply chain, which include reducing operational costs, improving inventory turnover, enhancing service levels, and ensuring timely delivery of products.

Key Factors in Warehousing and Distribution Strategy Design

To develop an effective warehousing and distribution strategy, businesses must consider a range of factors that directly impact operational efficiency, cost control, and customer service. These factors include:

Inventory Management: Effective inventory management is at the heart of both warehousing and distribution. Companies must decide on the appropriate inventory levels, stocking methods, and replenishment schedules to ensure that products are available when needed without overstocking or tying up excess capital in inventory. Key techniques include just-in-time (JIT), economic order quantity (EOQ), and safety stock strategies, which help optimize stock levels and reduce warehousing costs.

>**Location of Warehouses:** The geographical location of warehouses has a profound impact on the efficiency of the distribution process. Strategically placed warehouses can reduce transportation costs, improve lead times, and enhance customer service. Companies often evaluate factors such as proximity to major transportation routes, access to markets, and the availability of labor when selecting warehouse locations. Centralized versus decentralized warehouse models are also important considerations—centralized warehouses concentrate inventory in a single location, while decentralized warehouses distribute inventory across multiple sites to reduce delivery times.

>**Technology Integration:** Modern warehousing and distribution operations rely heavily on technology to streamline processes and increase efficiency. Warehouse management systems (WMS) are used to track inventory, manage order picking, and optimize the layout of storage areas. Barcode scanning, RFID (Radio Frequency Identification), and automation technologies such as robotic systems and conveyor belts also contribute to the efficiency of warehouses. In

distribution, technologies like GPS tracking, route optimization software, and automated sortation systems help businesses deliver products faster and at a lower cost.

Supply Chain Visibility: Real-time visibility into inventory levels, order status, and distribution activities allows businesses to proactively manage their supply chains. By utilizing technology such as cloud-based platforms and integrated systems, companies can gain end-to-end visibility of their operations, which is essential for managing demand fluctuations, improving decision-making, and addressing issues promptly.

Customer Expectations: With the growing demand for faster and more reliable delivery, customer expectations play a significant role in shaping warehousing and distribution strategies. Businesses must align their distribution strategies to meet customer expectations for speed, cost, and delivery accuracy. This may involve offering faster shipping options, free returns, and real-time tracking, all of which contribute to enhanced customer satisfaction.

Types of Warehousing Strategies

Various warehousing strategies can be employed based on business needs, operational goals, and customer requirements. Below are some of the most commonly used strategies:

Centralized Warehousing: In a centralized warehousing strategy, all inventory is stored in a single location, which can result in economies of scale and simplified inventory management. This model is suitable for companies with fewer or more predictable products that don't require frequent movement. It can help reduce overhead costs, but the primary trade-off is longer lead times for deliveries to customers located far from the warehouse.

Decentralized Warehousing: This strategy involves establishing multiple warehouse locations in different regions or markets to provide quicker access to customers and reduce transportation costs. Decentralized warehousing can help businesses offer faster delivery times, enhance regional customer service, and better accommodate demand spikes. However, it can lead to higher operational costs and complexity in inventory management.

Cross-Docking: Cross-docking is a highly efficient strategy that involves unloading goods from inbound transportation vehicles directly onto outbound vehicles with minimal or no storage time in the warehouse. The main objective of cross-docking is to speed up the flow of goods through the supply chain and reduce the need for extensive warehousing. This strategy is most beneficial for perishable goods, high-demand products, or goods that need to be quickly redistributed.

Automated Warehousing: The use of automation in warehouses, such as automated storage and retrieval systems (AS/RS), robotics, and conveyor systems, enhances the speed and accuracy of order fulfillment. Automated warehouses are particularly beneficial for businesses that handle large volumes of inventory, as they help reduce labor costs, increase throughput, and optimize space utilization.

Temperature-Controlled Warehousing: For industries dealing with perishable goods, pharmaceuticals, or sensitive materials, temperature-controlled warehousing is essential. This strategy involves the use of climate-controlled facilities that maintain specific temperature and humidity levels to ensure the integrity of products throughout storage. These warehouses typically utilize refrigeration or air conditioning systems and are monitored closely to maintain optimal conditions.

Types of Distribution Strategies

Once goods are stored and ready for dispatch, distribution strategies come into play. The selection of an appropriate distribution strategy depends on factors such as the nature of the product, delivery time requirements, geographic location of customers, and cost considerations. Some common distribution strategies include:

Direct Distribution (Direct-to-Consumer): This strategy involves sending products directly from the manufacturer or warehouse to the end consumer, bypassing intermediaries such as wholesalers or retailers. Direct distribution allows businesses to maintain greater control over the customer experience, reduce distribution costs, and provide faster delivery. This strategy is increasingly popular with e-commerce businesses, especially those that sell products online.

Indirect Distribution (Through Intermediaries): In contrast to direct distribution, indirect distribution involves using intermediaries such as wholesalers, retailers, and distributors to reach end consumers. This strategy is often employed by businesses looking to expand their reach into multiple geographic regions or markets without establishing their own distribution network. While this approach allows for wider market coverage, it may result in reduced profit margins due to reliance on intermediaries.

Omnichannel Distribution: With the rise of e-commerce, omnichannel distribution has become a popular strategy that integrates multiple channels, including brick-and-mortar stores, online platforms, and direct shipments. By offering customers various options for purchasing and receiving products, businesses can enhance the customer experience and provide flexibility. Omnichannel distribution enables companies to reach consumers wherever they prefer to shop, whether online or in-person, while also creating efficiencies in inventory management and fulfillment.

Third-Party Logistics (3PL): Third-party logistics providers offer outsourced services related to warehousing, distribution, and transportation. Companies often turn to 3PLs to reduce costs, increase operational efficiency, and gain access to advanced logistics technologies. 3PL providers handle everything from inventory management to order fulfillment, allowing businesses to focus on core competencies and scale their operations more effectively.

Fourth-Party Logistics (4PL): A more advanced version of 3PL, a fourth-party logistics provider takes on a more strategic role, managing the entire supply chain. A 4PL provider acts as a single point of contact for all logistics functions and can integrate various service providers to create a comprehensive logistics solution for a company. This strategy is suitable for businesses with complex supply chain needs, as it provides a holistic approach to supply chain management and maximizes efficiency across multiple touchpoints.

Key Considerations for Effective Warehousing and Distribution

Cost Management: One of the primary objectives of warehousing and distribution strategies is cost control. Businesses must carefully analyze warehousing costs, including rent, utilities, labor, and equipment, as well as distribution costs such as transportation and shipping fees. By implementing cost-effective strategies, such as optimizing warehouse layouts, utilizing energy-efficient equipment, and selecting the most suitable transportation modes, businesses can significantly reduce logistics expenses.

Customer Service: Ultimately, the goal of warehousing and distribution strategies is to enhance customer service. Speed, accuracy, and reliability of deliveries directly affect customer satisfaction and loyalty. By implementing flexible and responsive distribution systems, such as offering multiple shipping options, real-time order tracking, and efficient returns management, businesses can improve the overall customer experience.

Sustainability: Environmental considerations are becoming increasingly important in warehousing and distribution. Businesses are under pressure to reduce their carbon footprint and adopt more sustainable practices in logistics operations. This may involve utilizing energy-efficient warehouses, optimizing delivery routes to minimize fuel consumption, and adopting eco-friendly packaging materials. Companies that prioritize sustainability can not only reduce costs but also enhance their brand reputation.

Warehousing and distribution are essential functions of modern supply chain management. By developing and implementing effective warehousing and distribution strategies, businesses can optimize inventory management, reduce operational costs, and improve customer satisfaction. The choice of warehousing and distribution strategy depends on factors such as the nature of the product, market demands, delivery time requirements, and cost considerations. Whether employing centralized or decentralized warehousing, direct or indirect distribution, or leveraging third-party logistics, companies must ensure that their warehousing and distribution strategies align with their broader business objectives and the evolving demands of the market.

Cross-docking and Last-Mile Delivery

In the modern supply chain, ensuring the swift movement of goods from point A to point B is crucial. Two strategies that significantly influence the efficiency of the supply chain are **cross-docking** and **last-mile delivery**. Both of these strategies aim to improve the speed, reduce costs, and optimize the flow of goods, albeit at different stages of the distribution process. Together, they form a critical part of the logistics ecosystem, especially with the increasing demand for faster and more reliable delivery options in today's competitive market.

Cross-Docking: An Overview

Cross-docking is a logistics practice that involves unloading products from inbound transportation vehicles (such as trucks or containers) directly onto outbound vehicles with minimal or no storage time in between. The objective is to speed up the movement of goods through the supply chain, reducing storage costs and accelerating the overall delivery process. Cross-docking is particularly effective in scenarios where goods are required to be delivered quickly or when managing perishable or high-demand products.

Cross-docking operates on the principle of consolidating or distributing products as they arrive, allowing for immediate re-shipment without needing long-term storage in a warehouse. This process significantly reduces the handling time, inventory holding costs, and the need for extensive warehousing. Instead of storing goods in a traditional warehouse, cross-docking facilities act as temporary transfer points for products before they are quickly moved to their next destination. The effectiveness of cross-docking is measured by its ability to streamline the flow of goods, thereby enhancing the efficiency of the entire supply chain.

There are two primary types of cross-docking:

> **Pre-distribution Cross-docking:** This type is primarily used when the products are sorted based on orders before arriving at the facility. The items are then quickly directed to the appropriate outbound transportation channels. Pre-distribution is common for retail businesses or e-commerce operations where the inventory needs to be directed to various stores or customers.
>
> **Post-distribution Cross-docking:** In this method, products are unloaded, sorted, and consolidated after arriving at the dock,

then shipped out to customers or retailers. This method is often used in more complex supply chains where products may come from multiple suppliers or manufacturers and require further sorting.

The main advantage of cross-docking is its ability to reduce the time goods spend in transit and storage. In turn, this reduces handling costs, inventory costs, and the risk of stockouts or overstocking. Additionally, cross-docking supports just-in-time (JIT) inventory practices, where goods are delivered precisely when needed, preventing excess stock accumulation.

Benefits of Cross-Docking

Reduced Inventory Costs: Since goods are not stored for long periods, businesses can minimize the costs associated with warehousing, such as rent, insurance, and inventory holding costs.

Faster Delivery Times: Cross-docking minimizes the time products spend in transit, resulting in quicker delivery to customers or retailers. This is a significant advantage in industries where speed is crucial, such as perishable goods or e-commerce.

Lower Handling Costs: With fewer products being stored and moved over long distances within warehouses, handling costs are reduced. Products only go through the process of unloading, sorting, and immediate re-shipping.

Better Customer Satisfaction: By shortening the time it takes for products to reach their destination, cross-docking improves order fulfillment speed, which enhances customer satisfaction and strengthens the overall customer experience.

Efficient Use of Resources: Cross-docking allows businesses to utilize transportation resources more efficiently. For example, rather than sending multiple deliveries to various locations, goods can be consolidated and shipped together, reducing overall transportation costs.

Challenges of Cross-Docking

Despite its benefits, cross-docking is not without its challenges. It requires precise planning and coordination to ensure that products are correctly identified, sorted, and transferred efficiently between inbound and outbound shipments. Without effective technology systems, real-time tracking, and a clear understanding of supply and demand, the process can be chaotic and prone to errors.

Additionally, cross-docking may not be suitable for all types of products. For instance, products with a long shelf life or those that require significant sorting and inspection may not benefit from this process. Perishable goods, however, benefit most from cross-docking as it helps minimize the time they are in transit, which is critical for maintaining freshness.

Last-Mile Delivery: An Overview

The last mile refers to the final leg of the delivery process, where products are transported from a distribution center or local warehouse to the final customer or retailer. The last mile is the most crucial and costly part of the entire supply chain, often making up the bulk of the total transportation costs in logistics. As e-commerce continues to expand, the importance of last-mile delivery has grown significantly, particularly as customers increasingly demand faster and more convenient delivery options.

Unlike the broader transportation network, which may involve long-haul trucking and distribution centers, the last mile typically involves smaller vehicles like delivery vans, trucks, or even bicycles for urban areas. The focus is on getting the product into the hands of the customer as quickly, accurately, and cost-effectively as possible.

The challenges faced during the last mile delivery phase include traffic congestion, route optimization, delivery time windows, and the need for personalized delivery experiences. As businesses aim to meet customers' growing expectations for fast and affordable deliveries, companies are increasingly adopting innovative strategies and technologies to improve last-mile efficiency.

Last-Mile Delivery Strategies

Same-Day or Next-Day Delivery: With the rise of e-commerce giants such as Amazon, same-day or next-day delivery has become a highly sought-after service. Retailers and logistics providers are under pressure to meet these expectations. Efficient management of inventory and distribution centers, along with optimized last-mile logistics, is critical for delivering products on time.

Click-and-Collect: In this strategy, customers order products online and then pick them up at a designated collection point, such as a local store or a parcel locker. Click-and-collect services offer a more cost-effective alternative to home deliveries while still providing customers with the convenience of online shopping.

Crowdsourced Delivery: This method involves utilizing local individuals (or independent contractors) to deliver products directly to customers. By tapping into a network of crowdsourced drivers, businesses can reduce last-mile costs and achieve faster deliveries. Many companies, including those in the food delivery space, have adopted this approach to improve speed and reduce delivery costs.

Urban Delivery Hubs: To combat the challenges of city congestion and narrow streets, some companies have set up micro-warehouses or urban delivery hubs. These hubs act as distribution points within major cities, where products are stored temporarily before being delivered to customers. The idea is to reduce delivery times and transportation costs by getting products closer to the customer.

Drones and Autonomous Vehicles: As technology advances, drones and autonomous vehicles have begun to play a role in last-mile delivery. Drones can potentially deliver lightweight packages directly to customers, bypassing traffic congestion and reducing delivery times. Similarly, autonomous delivery vehicles have the potential to revolutionize last-mile delivery by cutting down on labor costs and increasing delivery efficiency.

Benefits of Efficient Last-Mile Delivery

Improved Customer Experience: Fast, reliable, and cost-effective last-mile delivery is crucial to enhancing customer satisfaction. The final delivery stage is often the most visible and impactful, and any delays or issues at this stage can negatively affect the entire shopping experience.

Cost Reduction: With efficient route planning, technology integration, and creative delivery solutions, businesses can reduce the overall cost of last-mile delivery, which has historically been the most expensive part of the supply chain.

Increased Competitiveness: In an environment where consumers increasingly value speed and convenience, companies with efficient last-mile delivery systems gain a competitive advantage. Businesses that can offer faster, cheaper, and more reliable deliveries often see greater customer loyalty and increased market share.

Environmental Benefits: Using electric vehicles, optimizing delivery routes, and adopting sustainable packaging are ways companies can reduce the environmental impact of last-mile deliveries. Sustainable last-mile solutions not only help reduce carbon emissions but also align with growing consumer demand for eco-friendly business practices.

Both **cross-docking** and **last-mile delivery** are essential components of modern logistics and supply chain management. Cross-docking accelerates the movement of goods by minimizing storage time and handling costs, while last-mile delivery focuses on efficiently getting products into the hands of customers. These strategies are central to meeting the rising demand for faster delivery times and enhancing the overall customer experience. As technology continues to evolve, businesses must remain agile, adopting new solutions that address the unique challenges of these critical stages in the supply chain. Ultimately, effective management of cross-docking and last-mile delivery can lead to significant cost savings, increased customer satisfaction, and a competitive edge in today's fast-paced global market.

Chapter 11: Technology in Supply Chain Management

Role of ERP and supply chain software.

In today's highly competitive and interconnected business environment, efficient supply chain management is crucial for the smooth operation of any organization. Businesses face increasing pressure to reduce costs, improve customer service, enhance decision-making capabilities, and maintain visibility across their supply chains. As supply chains become more complex, the role of technology, specifically Enterprise Resource Planning (ERP) systems and supply chain management software, has become more significant. These technological solutions help businesses optimize their processes, improve collaboration, and enhance the overall performance of their supply chains.

Enterprise Resource Planning (ERP) Systems: A Centralized Hub for Supply Chain Management

An **Enterprise Resource Planning (ERP) system** integrates core business processes and functions into a single unified platform. Traditionally, ERP systems were designed to manage back-office functions such as finance, human resources, and inventory control. However, over time, ERP systems have evolved to include modules that address various aspects of supply chain management (SCM), making them a powerful tool for businesses to improve operational efficiency across their entire supply chain.

ERP systems act as a centralized hub that connects all functions involved in the supply chain, including procurement, production, inventory management, logistics, and distribution. By using a single system to track and manage data, organizations can reduce the fragmentation of information that often occurs when different departments or systems are used. This centralized approach enables better visibility, communication, and decision-making across the supply chain, leading to improved coordination between departments and better alignment with organizational goals.

Key Features of ERP Systems in Supply Chain Management

Inventory Management: ERP systems provide businesses with real-time information on inventory levels, helping to minimize stockouts, reduce excess inventory, and improve demand forecasting. Accurate inventory tracking allows for efficient stock control, improving order fulfillment and reducing storage costs.

Procurement and Sourcing: ERP systems help streamline procurement processes by automating tasks such as supplier selection, purchase orders, and contract management. The system provides transparency in supplier performance, enabling better supplier relationships and more informed decisions.

Demand Forecasting and Planning: Many ERP systems include advanced forecasting capabilities, using historical data and trends to predict future demand. This helps businesses anticipate market fluctuations, optimize production schedules, and reduce the risk of overstocking or stockouts.

Production and Manufacturing Planning: ERP systems allow for better coordination between procurement and production teams, ensuring that materials and components are available when needed. The system can track production schedules, monitor manufacturing progress, and manage resources efficiently, reducing waste and improving productivity.

Logistics and Distribution: ERP systems help manage the logistics of delivering goods to customers by optimizing transportation routes, managing distribution centers, and automating shipping schedules. They also provide real-time visibility into order status, improving communication with customers and reducing delivery delays.

Financial Integration: ERP systems integrate supply chain functions with financial data, helping businesses manage costs, track expenses, and optimize financial performance. The system can provide insights into procurement costs, inventory turnover, and overall profitability, enabling more informed decision-making.

Benefits of ERP in Supply Chain Management

Improved Visibility and Control: By consolidating data across the supply chain, ERP systems provide businesses with real-time visibility into inventory, orders, suppliers, and shipments. This improved visibility enables better decision-making and allows businesses to respond quickly to changes in demand, disruptions, or supply chain risks.

Enhanced Efficiency: ERP systems automate repetitive tasks such as order processing, invoicing, and inventory tracking, reducing the need for manual intervention. This improves operational efficiency, reduces errors, and frees up resources for more strategic activities.

Better Collaboration: The integrated nature of ERP systems fosters collaboration between different departments within an organization. Procurement teams, inventory managers, production planners, and logistics staff can access the same data in real time, improving coordination and reducing the risk of miscommunication or delays.

Scalability and Flexibility: As businesses grow, ERP systems can scale to accommodate new locations, products, and suppliers. The modular nature of many ERP systems allows organizations to add new functionalities as needed, providing flexibility to adapt to changing business requirements.

Cost Reduction: By improving inventory management, reducing waste, optimizing procurement, and enhancing production scheduling, ERP systems help businesses reduce operational costs. The ability to track and control expenses across the supply chain also leads to better financial management and profitability.

Supply Chain Management (SCM) Software: Specialized Solutions for Enhanced Supply Chain Efficiency

While ERP systems provide a broad solution for managing business processes, **supply chain management (SCM) software** is a more specialized category of software that focuses specifically on optimizing the supply chain. SCM software includes a range of tools and solutions designed to improve specific areas of the supply chain, from demand forecasting to transportation management. These solutions often integrate with ERP systems but provide additional features tailored to the complexities of supply chain operations.

Key Types of Supply Chain Software

Transportation Management Systems (TMS): TMS software focuses on optimizing the transportation of goods throughout the supply chain. It helps businesses plan, execute, and monitor shipments, improve route planning, reduce fuel costs, and ensure timely deliveries. TMS also provides real-time tracking, allowing businesses to monitor the status of shipments and react quickly to potential delays or disruptions.

Warehouse Management Systems (WMS): WMS software helps manage the operations of a warehouse, including inventory tracking, order picking, packing, and shipping. WMS solutions improve warehouse efficiency by automating processes such as stock control, order fulfillment, and space optimization, reducing human error and improving order accuracy.

Demand Planning and Forecasting Software: This software helps businesses predict future demand by analyzing historical sales data, market trends, and other variables. Advanced forecasting models can use machine learning and artificial intelligence (AI) to improve accuracy and provide more reliable insights into demand fluctuations.

Supplier Relationship Management (SRM): SRM software helps businesses manage relationships with suppliers by automating tasks such as supplier selection, performance evaluation, and contract management. SRM solutions allow businesses to track supplier performance, identify potential risks, and collaborate more effectively with suppliers to improve product quality and delivery reliability.

Order Management Systems (OMS): OMS software helps businesses manage customer orders from start to finish. It includes tools for order tracking, inventory allocation, and order fulfillment. OMS ensures that orders are processed efficiently and that inventory is available when needed to meet customer demand.

Advanced Planning and Scheduling (APS): APS software helps optimize production scheduling and resource allocation. By considering constraints such as labor, materials, and machinery, APS solutions help businesses maximize production efficiency, minimize downtime, and ensure that products are delivered on time.

Benefits of SCM Software

Enhanced Decision-Making: SCM software provides businesses with real-time data and analytics, enabling managers to make more informed decisions. This data-driven approach allows for better demand forecasting, inventory management, and production planning.

Improved Supplier and Customer Collaboration: SCM software fosters collaboration between businesses and their suppliers or customers. By providing visibility into inventory levels, order status, and delivery schedules, businesses can build stronger relationships with suppliers and provide better service to customers.

Increased Flexibility and Responsiveness: With the ability to track and manage shipments, monitor inventory, and respond to changes in demand, SCM software allows businesses to be more agile and responsive to disruptions or changes in the market.

Cost Savings: By optimizing processes such as transportation, inventory management, and supplier relationships, SCM software helps businesses reduce costs and improve profitability. It enables businesses to identify inefficiencies, reduce waste, and improve overall supply chain performance.

Improved Customer Service: With accurate demand forecasting, better inventory control, and streamlined order fulfillment, SCM software helps businesses meet customer expectations for product availability, delivery speed, and order accuracy.

Integration of ERP and SCM Software for Seamless Supply Chain Operations

While ERP and SCM software can be used independently, the true power of these technologies is realized when they are integrated. Integration allows businesses to streamline operations, improve data accuracy, and enhance visibility across the entire supply chain. For example, integrating an ERP system with a TMS can provide end-to-end visibility into inventory levels, order status, and transportation schedules, enabling businesses to optimize their logistics and improve customer service.

By leveraging both ERP and SCM software, businesses can gain a comprehensive view of their supply chain, from procurement to distribution. This integrated approach enables better decision-making, more efficient operations, and a more agile supply chain that can adapt to changing market conditions.

The role of ERP and supply chain software in modern supply chain management cannot be overstated. These technologies help businesses optimize operations, improve decision-making, and reduce costs while providing better visibility and control over the entire supply chain. As businesses face increasing pressure to meet customer demands for faster, more reliable deliveries, the integration of ERP and SCM software will continue to play a critical role in driving supply chain efficiency and competitive advantage. By adopting and effectively utilizing these technologies, organizations can streamline their processes, enhance collaboration, and improve overall supply chain performance.

Impact of IoT, AI, and Blockchain on Supply Chains

The supply chain landscape is undergoing a transformation driven by technological advancements. Among the most influential technologies reshaping modern supply chains are the Internet of Things (IoT), Artificial Intelligence (AI), and Blockchain. These technologies offer unparalleled opportunities to enhance supply chain efficiency, transparency, and resilience, and they are driving new levels of automation, optimization, and trust. The integration of these technologies into supply chain operations is helping organizations tackle challenges such as cost reduction, demand forecasting, supply chain visibility, and fraud prevention, ultimately transforming the way businesses operate.

The Internet of Things (IoT) and its Impact on Supply Chains

The **Internet of Things (IoT)** refers to the network of physical objects, devices, and systems embedded with sensors, software, and connectivity, allowing them to collect, exchange, and analyze data. IoT has a profound impact on supply chains by enhancing visibility, improving decision-making, and driving automation.

Enhanced Visibility and Tracking

IoT enables real-time monitoring of goods, vehicles, and equipment across the entire supply chain. Sensors embedded in products or containers allow businesses to track the location, condition, and status of shipments at every stage of their journey. For example, IoT-enabled tracking devices can provide data on the temperature of perishable goods during transport, ensuring that they are kept within safe conditions. In the case of high-value assets, IoT allows for continuous location monitoring, reducing the risk of theft and enhancing security.

Additionally, warehouse management systems (WMS) integrated with IoT sensors enable organizations to monitor inventory levels, automate stock replenishment, and optimize space utilization within the warehouse. IoT can also track the movement of materials through production lines, ensuring that they are used efficiently, reducing waste, and improving throughput.

Improved Predictive Maintenance

IoT devices can monitor the condition of critical machinery and equipment in the supply chain, such as conveyors, trucks, or manufacturing plants. By collecting data on factors like temperature, vibration, and wear, IoT systems can predict when equipment is likely to fail and schedule maintenance before breakdowns occur. This predictive maintenance capability minimizes downtime, extends the lifespan of equipment, and reduces repair costs.

Optimization of Routes and Logistics

IoT-enabled GPS systems can optimize transportation routes in real time, taking into account traffic, weather conditions, and other factors. This reduces fuel consumption, improves delivery times, and decreases the environmental impact of transportation. By using IoT to monitor fleet performance, businesses can enhance logistics planning, reduce inefficiencies, and improve customer satisfaction with more accurate delivery estimates.

Artificial Intelligence (AI) and its Impact on Supply Chains

Artificial Intelligence (AI) refers to machines and systems that simulate human intelligence to analyze data, recognize patterns, and make decisions. AI has the potential to revolutionize supply chains by enabling automation, improving forecasting accuracy, enhancing customer service, and optimizing decision-making processes.

Demand Forecasting and Inventory Optimization

One of the key applications of AI in supply chains is **demand forecasting**. AI algorithms, particularly machine learning (ML), can analyze vast amounts of historical data, market trends, and external factors (such as weather or economic indicators) to predict future demand. AI systems continuously learn from new data, improving their predictions over time, which helps businesses reduce stockouts and overstocking, optimize inventory levels, and improve customer satisfaction.

AI also plays a critical role in **inventory optimization**. By analyzing real-time sales data and customer behavior, AI systems can recommend optimal inventory levels, suggest reordering schedules, and even predict changes in customer demand. This allows companies to maintain leaner inventories while minimizing the risk of stockouts.

Automation of Repetitive Tasks

AI can automate many repetitive and time-consuming tasks in supply chain management, such as order processing, invoice reconciliation, and supplier management. Robotic Process Automation (RPA) combined with AI can handle administrative tasks, reducing human error, improving efficiency, and enabling employees to focus on more strategic activities.

For example, AI-powered chatbots can handle customer service inquiries regarding order status or inventory availability. This enhances the customer experience by providing immediate responses and reducing the need for human intervention. Similarly, AI can automate procurement processes by identifying suitable suppliers, analyzing bids, and recommending purchasing decisions based on historical data and performance metrics.

Optimization of Production and Distribution

AI-driven algorithms can also optimize production scheduling by analyzing available resources, machine capacities, and production timelines. By dynamically adjusting schedules in response to changes in demand or supply chain disruptions, AI helps ensure that production lines are always operating at optimal capacity.

In distribution, AI can optimize warehouse picking strategies, improving the speed and accuracy of order fulfillment. For instance, AI-powered robots and drones can assist in locating and picking inventory items, improving the efficiency of warehouse operations and reducing labor costs.

Risk Management and Decision Support

AI can analyze risk factors across the supply chain and provide real-time decision support. For example, AI systems can detect anomalies in data, such as sudden spikes in demand or supply disruptions, and recommend corrective actions. By providing managers with actionable insights, AI helps mitigate risks and prevent costly disruptions, enhancing the resilience of the supply chain.

Blockchain and its Impact on Supply Chains

Blockchain technology is a decentralized digital ledger that records transactions across multiple computers in such a way that the registered transactions cannot be altered retroactively. The **immutable** nature of blockchain provides transparency, traceability, and security, making it a powerful tool for improving trust and reducing fraud in supply chains.

Improved Transparency and Traceability

Blockchain enables end-to-end transparency in the supply chain by recording every transaction (e.g., shipment, payment, or transfer of goods) on a public ledger. This provides all stakeholders, including suppliers, manufacturers, and customers, with access to the same information, ensuring that all parties have visibility into the movement of goods and associated transactions.

For example, a product's journey can be traced from its origin to the final customer. In industries such as food, pharmaceuticals, and luxury goods, this level of transparency is especially critical. Blockchain ensures that products have not been tampered with during transit and provides consumers with confidence in the quality and authenticity of the products they purchase.

Enhancing Supply Chain Security

Blockchain's decentralized and tamper-proof nature enhances the security of supply chain transactions. Traditional supply chains often involve multiple intermediaries and paper-based systems, which can be vulnerable to fraud, data manipulation, or cyberattacks. Blockchain, with its cryptographic security, reduces the likelihood of fraud and ensures that data integrity is maintained throughout the supply chain process.

For instance, smart contracts—self-executing contracts with predefined conditions—can be used to automate payment processes, ensuring that payments are only made when goods are delivered or conditions are met. This reduces the risk of fraud and minimizes the need for intermediaries.

Faster and More Efficient Transactions

Blockchain can speed up transaction processing times by eliminating intermediaries and reducing the complexity of verification processes. In a traditional supply chain, the verification of payments, deliveries, and contracts may involve multiple parties and take several days to complete. Blockchain enables real-time validation, reducing delays and ensuring faster processing of payments and transactions.

Reducing Counterfeiting and Ensuring Product Quality

In industries prone to counterfeiting, such as pharmaceuticals, automotive parts, and electronics, blockchain offers an effective solution to combat the issue. By recording every step in the product's journey, from raw material sourcing to final delivery, blockchain can help verify the authenticity of products and prevent counterfeit goods from entering the supply chain.

For example, the pharmaceutical industry has implemented blockchain to track the movement of drugs through the supply chain, ensuring that counterfeit medicines are not distributed to consumers. Similarly, in the luxury goods market, blockchain helps ensure that high-value items, such as watches and handbags, are genuine and not counterfeit.

The Synergy of IoT, AI, and Blockchain

The true potential of IoT, AI, and blockchain is realized when these technologies are integrated into a cohesive ecosystem. Each technology brings unique capabilities to the supply chain, and when combined, they create a more intelligent, efficient, and resilient supply chain.

For instance, IoT devices can gather real-time data from shipments and production lines, which can then be analyzed by AI algorithms to make more accurate forecasts or optimize operations. Blockchain can provide a secure and transparent platform for recording these transactions, ensuring data integrity and enhancing trust.

Together, these technologies enable businesses to achieve a higher level of automation, optimize decision-making, improve collaboration, and build more resilient supply chains that can adapt to disruptions, changes in demand, and other challenges.

Conclusion

The impact of IoT, AI, and blockchain on supply chains is transformative, driving significant improvements in efficiency, transparency, and security. These technologies are reshaping how businesses operate, offering enhanced visibility, automation, and real-time decision-making capabilities. As supply chains become more complex and global, the integration of IoT, AI, and blockchain will continue to play a pivotal role in enabling businesses to stay competitive, meet customer demands, and build more resilient supply chains. Organizations that successfully leverage these technologies will be better positioned to navigate the challenges of the modern business environment and achieve long-term success.

Part 4: Sustainable and Resilient Supply Chains

Chapter 12: Sustainable Procurement

Sustainability has become a crucial driver in global business practices, and procurement is no exception. Sustainable procurement focuses on the strategic integration of environmental, social, and economic considerations into procurement activities. The aim is to create a more responsible and ethical supply chain that not only meets the immediate needs of an organization but also supports long-term environmental and social goals. This approach ensures that procurement decisions contribute to minimizing environmental impact, fostering social responsibility, and promoting economic sustainability.

Green Procurement Strategies

Green procurement, often referred to as environmentally sustainable procurement, emphasizes the acquisition of goods and services that have a minimal impact on the environment. This strategy requires organizations to consider environmental factors across the entire product lifecycle, from raw material extraction to end-of-life disposal. The ultimate goal of green procurement is to minimize carbon footprints, conserve resources, reduce waste, and promote environmental sustainability within the supply chain.

1. Energy Efficiency and Carbon Reduction

One of the key components of green procurement is the selection of suppliers and products that contribute to energy efficiency and carbon footprint reduction. Organizations are increasingly focusing on procuring products that consume less energy during production and use, or those that are energy-efficient in their final application. For example, businesses may opt to source energy-efficient machinery, appliances, or vehicles that consume less power during operation, thereby reducing overall emissions.

In transportation, green procurement can involve selecting low-emission vehicles or logistics partners that prioritize fuel-efficient fleets. Similarly, companies might select renewable energy sources for their operations, such as solar or wind energy, to power factories and facilities, further reducing their carbon footprint.

2. Resource Conservation and Waste Reduction

Another critical aspect of green procurement is the emphasis on resource conservation. This involves sourcing products made from renewable resources, recyclable materials, or sustainably sourced raw materials. Companies committed to sustainability often demand that their suppliers use environmentally friendly materials, such as recycled content or biodegradable substances, in the production of goods.

For example, packaging waste is a significant issue in many industries, and green procurement strategies include adopting materials that are recyclable, compostable, or reusable, which reduces waste sent to landfills. Additionally, procurement teams are increasingly favoring products that have a longer lifespan, as they help reduce the need for frequent replacements, further lowering resource consumption and waste generation.

3. Eco-Design and Circular Economy

Eco-design is another critical element of green procurement. This approach encourages the design of products with the environment in mind, ensuring that products are created with minimal environmental impact from the outset. Products that are designed with eco-friendly materials, energy-efficient features, and easy recyclability help reduce the environmental footprint across their lifecycle.

The circular economy is closely related to eco-design. Instead of following the traditional linear model of production, consumption, and disposal, the circular economy aims to create closed-loop systems where products and materials are reused, refurbished, or recycled. Organizations embracing sustainable procurement can support this model by procuring products designed for easy disassembly and recycling, facilitating product life extension and minimizing waste.

4. Certification and Standards for Green Procurement

To ensure credibility and standardization, many organizations adhere to internationally recognized sustainability certifications and standards. These certifications validate that products and services meet specific environmental criteria. Popular green certifications include Energy Star, Fair Trade, Forest Stewardship Council (FSC), and the Global Organic Textile Standard (GOTS), among others.

By sourcing products with these certifications, organizations ensure that they are procuring goods and services that have undergone rigorous environmental or social assessments. Furthermore, adopting these standards can help organizations align their procurement strategies with global sustainability goals, particularly those outlined in frameworks like the United Nations Sustainable Development Goals (SDGs).

5. Collaboration with Sustainable Suppliers

A key success factor in green procurement is building strong, long-term relationships with suppliers that prioritize sustainability. Procurement departments increasingly seek to partner with suppliers who have demonstrated a commitment to environmental stewardship, social responsibility, and ethical business practices. Collaborating with such suppliers allows organizations to collectively address sustainability challenges and create innovative solutions that can further reduce environmental impact.

Building these partnerships often requires organizations to engage in transparent communication and joint problem-solving. Suppliers can play an essential role in helping companies meet their sustainability targets, whether through the adoption of cleaner technologies, innovative product designs, or sustainable sourcing practices.

Environmental and Social Governance (ESG) in Procurement

Environmental and Social Governance (ESG) refers to the integration of environmental, social, and governance factors into business decision-making. ESG criteria are becoming a critical aspect of procurement strategies, influencing both the selection of suppliers and the evaluation of products and services. These criteria go beyond traditional financial metrics and focus on long-term value creation through responsible, ethical, and sustainable practices.

1. Environmental Governance in Procurement

Environmental governance addresses the environmental impact of business operations and the products or services that a company procures. This includes factors such as reducing carbon emissions, managing waste, conserving resources, and ensuring that products are sourced from environmentally responsible suppliers.

For example, organizations might incorporate environmental criteria into their supplier selection processes, such as requiring suppliers to comply with environmental regulations or to adopt carbon reduction practices. In some cases, organizations may even seek to work with suppliers who are leaders in sustainability and environmental stewardship, thereby enhancing their own environmental performance.

Incorporating environmental governance into procurement processes also involves understanding the broader environmental impact of supply chains, particularly in industries that have significant environmental footprints. For instance, companies in the apparel or electronics sectors may require suppliers to minimize water usage, reduce chemical emissions, or ensure the ethical sourcing of materials such as timber, cotton, or metals.

2. Social Governance in Procurement

Social governance focuses on the ethical and social dimensions of business operations. In procurement, this means evaluating suppliers based on their adherence to fair labor practices, human rights, health and safety standards, and community engagement. Ethical procurement practices prioritize suppliers who promote good working conditions, fair wages, and respect for workers' rights.

For example, procurement teams may choose to source products from suppliers who ensure that their workers receive fair wages, work in safe environments, and are treated with dignity and respect. In the context of global supply chains, social governance becomes particularly important, as it helps mitigate risks associated with unethical practices such as child labor, forced labor, or unsafe working conditions.

Furthermore, companies are increasingly focusing on supplier diversity as part of their social governance strategy. This involves actively seeking to engage with minority-owned, women-owned, and disadvantaged suppliers to promote inclusivity and equity within the supply chain.

3. Governance and Ethical Procurement Practices

The governance aspect of ESG in procurement ensures that organizations are held accountable for their supply chain decisions. It includes establishing policies and procedures for ethical procurement practices, ensuring transparency in sourcing, and mitigating risks related to corruption or fraud.

Governance in procurement also involves the oversight of supplier compliance with ethical and legal standards. Organizations can enhance governance by adopting codes of conduct, conducting regular audits, and establishing clear guidelines for supplier behavior. By doing so, they not only protect themselves from reputational damage but also contribute to a broader culture of ethical business practices.

4. ESG Reporting and Performance Metrics

As ESG considerations continue to gain importance, organizations are increasingly required to report on their sustainability and social governance efforts. ESG reporting provides stakeholders, including investors, customers, and regulators, with transparent information about a company's environmental, social, and governance performance.

In procurement, ESG reporting may include metrics related to the sustainability of products sourced, supplier diversity, the reduction of carbon emissions, waste management, and the ethical treatment of workers. By setting measurable ESG goals and reporting on progress, companies can demonstrate their commitment to responsible procurement practices and continuously improve their performance.

Sustainable procurement, driven by green procurement strategies and a commitment to environmental and social governance (ESG), is no longer just a trend but a critical business imperative. As companies face increasing pressure from consumers, investors, and regulators to adopt sustainable and responsible practices, procurement plays a pivotal role in driving these changes. By integrating sustainability into procurement decisions and supplier relationships, organizations can not only reduce their environmental impact but also create value through ethical, responsible sourcing practices that benefit society and the global economy.

As the demand for sustainable products and services grows, businesses must continue to evolve their procurement strategies to meet these expectations. By adopting green procurement strategies, fostering social governance, and aligning with ESG principles, procurement departments can contribute to building resilient, sustainable supply chains that deliver long-term value to both organizations and the world.

Circular Supply Chain Concepts

The concept of a circular supply chain represents a transformative approach to traditional linear supply chain models. In a linear supply chain, the typical flow follows a "take, make, dispose" pattern, where raw materials are extracted, used to create products, and ultimately discarded after use. This model often leads to significant environmental degradation, resource depletion, and waste accumulation. In contrast, a circular supply chain seeks to break this cycle by emphasizing the reuse, recycling, and regeneration of materials and products throughout their lifecycle. The ultimate goal of a circular supply chain is to create a closed-loop system, where products, materials, and resources are continuously cycled back into the economy, reducing waste and the consumption of finite resources.

The shift towards circular supply chains is driven by several factors, including growing concerns over sustainability, resource scarcity, and environmental impacts. Businesses are increasingly recognizing the importance of adopting circular principles in order to reduce their ecological footprint, create more efficient operations, and meet consumer demand for sustainable products and services. The rise of circular supply chains aligns with global sustainability agendas, including the United Nations' Sustainable Development Goals (SDGs), and is considered a vital component of creating a more resilient and responsible business ecosystem.

Core Principles of Circular Supply Chains

Circular supply chains are based on several key principles that help to redefine how products and materials are sourced, used, and disposed of. These principles include:

1. Design for Longevity and Durability

One of the central tenets of a circular supply chain is the design of products for longevity. Instead of creating products that are designed to be disposable or that have a short useful life, circular supply chains prioritize the creation of durable, long-lasting products that can be used and reused over time. This involves selecting materials that are resilient and that have the potential to be recycled or refurbished at the end of their life cycle.

For instance, businesses in the electronics industry may design products with modular components that can be easily repaired or upgraded, extending the lifespan of the product and reducing the need for frequent replacements. In the apparel industry, the design of clothing using sustainable fabrics and techniques that allow for easy recycling helps reduce waste and encourage circularity.

2. Product Life Extension

Product life extension is another crucial component of circular supply chains. It focuses on maximizing the lifespan of products through repair, refurbishment, and remanufacturing processes. Rather than products being discarded once they no longer function or meet consumer needs, they are restored to working condition and given a second life.

The practice of remanufacturing, for example, involves taking used or worn-out products, disassembling them, and restoring individual parts to like-new condition before reassembling them into fully functional products. This reduces the need for new raw materials, lowers waste, and reduces environmental impact. Automotive industries, for instance, use remanufacturing extensively for components like engines, batteries, and transmissions, which can be refurbished multiple times before they are eventually recycled.

3. Recycling and Resource Recovery

Recycling is a cornerstone of circular supply chains, as it focuses on recovering valuable materials from products that have reached the end of their life cycle. Rather than throwing products away, the materials within them—whether metals, plastics, textiles, or electronics—are extracted and returned to the production process. This reduces reliance on virgin resources, conserves natural capital, and minimizes waste that would otherwise end up in landfills.

Advanced recycling technologies, such as chemical recycling for plastics, are transforming industries by allowing the recovery of high-quality materials that can be used to make new products. Electronics manufacturers are also adopting methods for recovering rare earth metals, which are often used in high-tech components, ensuring that these valuable resources can be reused in the manufacturing of new devices.

4. Circular Business Models

Businesses that adopt circular supply chains often embrace new business models that prioritize product-as-a-service rather than ownership. Instead of selling products outright, companies may offer products on a rental, leasing, or subscription basis. For example, companies in industries such as fashion, electronics, and furniture are increasingly adopting business models that allow consumers to rent or lease products, ensuring that these items are returned for reuse, repair, or refurbishment after their life cycle.

The product-as-a-service model not only encourages sustainability but also fosters long-term customer relationships and offers companies opportunities to generate recurring revenue. For instance, car manufacturers may offer vehicles on lease, ensuring that vehicles are returned after a certain period for maintenance, upgrading, or resale. This allows the manufacturer to reclaim the car, refurbish it, and put it back into circulation, rather than allowing it to become waste.

5. Closed-Loop Logistics and Reverse Logistics

An essential aspect of a circular supply chain is the establishment of closed-loop logistics, or reverse logistics, which is focused on the efficient return of products and materials to the supply chain for reuse, recycling, or remanufacturing. Reverse logistics involves the collection of used products from customers, retailers, or other points in the supply chain, and returning them to the manufacturer or appropriate recycling facility.

Reverse logistics can be complex due to the need for reverse transportation, storage, sorting, and inspection of returned goods. However, businesses that implement efficient reverse logistics systems can recover valuable materials, reduce waste, and generate cost savings in the long term. Additionally, reverse logistics helps to meet customer expectations for sustainability by offering easy and convenient return options for products that can no longer be used.

6. Supply Chain Transparency and Collaboration

Circular supply chains also rely on transparency and collaboration among supply chain partners. Transparency involves ensuring that all actors in the supply chain are aware of the sustainability practices of their suppliers, the sourcing of raw materials, and the environmental impact of production. With transparent supply chains, businesses can ensure that their sourcing practices align with their sustainability goals.

Collaboration across the supply chain is essential for the successful implementation of circular principles. By working together, suppliers, manufacturers, retailers, and consumers can share information, exchange best practices, and collaborate on innovations that further circularity. For example, companies in the fashion industry may collaborate with recycling firms to ensure that textiles are properly recycled, or they may partner with product designers to create garments that are easier to recycle at the end of their life cycle.

Benefits of Circular Supply Chains

Circular supply chains offer numerous benefits to businesses, consumers, and society as a whole. These benefits include:

1. Environmental Benefits

By reducing waste, conserving natural resources, and promoting the reuse and recycling of materials, circular supply chains help to significantly lower environmental impact. They contribute to reducing carbon emissions, mitigating climate change, and promoting biodiversity. As businesses transition from linear to circular supply chains, they contribute to the global effort to create a more sustainable, regenerative economy.

2. Cost Savings and Resource Efficiency

Circular supply chains help businesses reduce costs by minimizing the need for raw materials, reducing waste disposal expenses, and optimizing the use of existing resources. The reuse and remanufacturing of products can also help lower production costs, as businesses can rely on secondary materials that are often cheaper than raw materials.

3. Enhanced Brand Image and Consumer Loyalty

Consumers are increasingly aware of the environmental and social impacts of their purchasing decisions. Businesses that embrace circular supply chains and promote sustainability can enhance their brand image and build loyalty among eco-conscious consumers. Circular practices help demonstrate a company's commitment to sustainability, which can attract new customers and strengthen relationships with existing ones.

4. Regulatory Compliance

As governments around the world impose stricter regulations related to waste management, emissions, and resource use, circular supply chains help businesses comply with these regulations. Adopting circular practices not only ensures compliance but also positions companies as leaders in sustainability, which can result in incentives such as tax breaks, government support, or enhanced market access.

Challenges of Circular Supply Chains

While circular supply chains offer significant benefits, there are also challenges associated with their implementation. These challenges include:

1. High Initial Investment

Transitioning from a linear to a circular supply chain often requires significant investment in new technologies, infrastructure, and training. Businesses may need to invest in advanced recycling systems, remanufacturing facilities, or reverse logistics networks, which can incur high upfront costs.

2. Supply Chain Complexity

Circular supply chains can be more complex to manage than traditional linear supply chains due to the need for greater coordination among multiple stakeholders. The involvement of recycling, remanufacturing, and reverse logistics requires companies to work closely with suppliers, customers, and recycling partners, which can lead to operational challenges.

3. Consumer Behavior

For circular supply chains to function effectively, consumers must be willing to return products for reuse or recycling. However, consumer behavior and perceptions of recycling, waste reduction, and sustainability can vary widely. Encouraging customers to participate in return programs or embrace product-as-a-service models requires substantial education and marketing efforts.

Circular supply chains represent a critical shift toward more sustainable business practices. By embracing principles such as product life extension, recycling, and closed-loop logistics, businesses can significantly reduce their environmental impact while creating economic value. While challenges remain, the benefits of circular supply chains, including cost savings, enhanced brand loyalty, and regulatory compliance, make them an essential part of the future of supply chain management. As the demand for sustainable practices continues to rise, circular supply chains will play a central role in creating a more resilient and responsible global economy.

Chapter 13: Building Resilient Supply Chains

In an increasingly interconnected and complex global marketplace, supply chains face a wide array of risks and potential disruptions that can severely impact operations. Events such as natural disasters, geopolitical instability, global pandemics, technological failures, and supply shortages can cause significant interruptions in the flow of goods, materials, and services. Given these challenges, it has become more critical than ever for businesses to build resilient supply chains capable of adapting to and recovering from such disruptions.

A resilient supply chain is one that can absorb shocks, recover from setbacks, and continue delivering products and services with minimal delays and costs. Building such a supply chain involves not only risk management strategies but also proactive measures to strengthen the supply chain's flexibility, adaptability, and response capabilities. The aim is to ensure continuity of operations, protect customer satisfaction, and safeguard the business from long-term disruptions.

Managing Disruptions and Risks

To build resilient supply chains, it is essential first to understand the types of disruptions and risks that may arise. These risks are typically categorized into the following:

1. External Risks

External risks are factors that are beyond the control of the supply chain organization but can significantly impact its operations. These include:

> **Natural Disasters:** Earthquakes, floods, hurricanes, wildfires, and other natural calamities can destroy infrastructure, disrupt transportation, and halt production, particularly in regions where supply chain networks are concentrated.

Geopolitical Risks: Political instability, trade wars, sanctions, and regulatory changes can disrupt the flow of goods, leading to delays and increased costs. This is especially relevant for global supply chains that rely on international trade.

Economic Shifts: Economic recessions, inflation, changes in consumer demand, or fluctuations in currency exchange rates can cause shifts in market conditions, making it harder to predict supply and demand trends accurately.

Pandemics and Health Crises: As seen with the COVID-19 pandemic, global health crises can disrupt supply chains by reducing workforce availability, restricting transportation, and altering demand for certain products.

2. Internal Risks

Internal risks stem from within the organization or supply chain itself and often relate to operational inefficiencies. These include:

Supply Shortages: A lack of critical raw materials, components, or finished goods can halt production, especially if suppliers experience disruptions or fail to meet delivery timelines.

Technological Failures: System outages, software malfunctions, or cyberattacks can disrupt operations, particularly for supply chains that rely heavily on digital systems for tracking, communication, and logistics.

Labor Issues: Strikes, workforce shortages, and challenges in labor management can disrupt supply chain operations, especially in sectors where specialized skills are needed, or labor shortages impact manufacturing and distribution.

Supplier Failure: The failure of key suppliers, whether due to financial difficulties, quality issues, or logistical challenges, can have ripple effects throughout the supply chain.

3. Demand and Supply Variability

Both demand and supply uncertainties pose significant risks. These risks arise from unpredictable consumer demand patterns, seasonal fluctuations, supply bottlenecks, or the sudden loss of a supplier. Managing demand and supply variability is a core component of supply chain resilience.

4. Financial Risks

Fluctuations in costs, credit risks, or the financial health of suppliers and customers can impact cash flow and profitability. Businesses that rely on complex financial arrangements, such as trade credit, factoring, or financing, may face liquidity problems in the event of disruptions.

Strategies for Supply Chain Resilience

To address these risks and build a resilient supply chain, companies need to implement strategic measures that help them better absorb disruptions, reduce their impacts, and recover quickly when necessary. Below are key strategies that can be employed to enhance supply chain resilience:

1. Diversification of Suppliers and Sourcing Locations

One of the most effective ways to manage supply chain risks is through supplier diversification. Relying on a single supplier or region for critical raw materials or components creates a single point of failure that can lead to significant disruptions in the event of a problem.

To reduce this risk, businesses should consider sourcing from multiple suppliers or diversifying their supplier base across different geographical locations. This ensures that if one supplier or region faces disruption, the business can pivot to other suppliers, thus maintaining continuity in operations. Additionally, businesses can look for nearshoring opportunities, bringing suppliers closer to home to reduce transportation risks, as well as reduce lead times and improve control over the supply process.

2. Building Strong Relationships with Suppliers

Beyond diversification, it is crucial to build strong, collaborative relationships with key suppliers. A well-established relationship allows for more effective communication and problem-solving during times of crisis. Suppliers are more likely to prioritize customers they have long-term relationships with, especially in situations where resources are limited or demand exceeds supply.

Supply chain managers should engage in regular discussions with suppliers to understand their capabilities, potential risks they face, and their contingency plans. This collaboration helps businesses develop mutual plans for managing disruptions, such as shared risk mitigation strategies, joint inventory planning, or joint forecasting.

3. Real-Time Data and Visibility

In today's fast-paced supply chain environment, having access to real-time data is critical for managing disruptions. Implementing supply chain visibility tools, such as advanced analytics, tracking systems, and dashboards, enables companies to monitor inventory levels, shipments, and supplier performance continuously.

Real-time data can help businesses quickly identify potential issues and take corrective actions before they escalate into significant problems. For example, if there is a disruption in transportation due to weather conditions, supply chain managers can use tracking systems to reroute shipments or shift to alternative modes of transport to minimize delays.

Incorporating Internet of Things (IoT) devices and sensors into supply chains also enhances visibility, enabling businesses to track the location, condition, and status of goods in transit or stored in warehouses. This data is invaluable when responding to disruptions, as it provides insight into exactly where issues are occurring, allowing for faster decision-making.

4. Inventory Buffering and Safety Stock

Maintaining appropriate levels of inventory is a traditional yet effective strategy for mitigating risks associated with supply chain disruptions. By holding safety stock or buffer inventory, companies can absorb temporary disruptions in supply or demand without immediate production stoppages.

However, this strategy must be balanced against the cost of carrying inventory. Companies need to analyze their supply chain risks and determine optimal safety stock levels based on factors such as lead time, supplier reliability, and demand variability. While excess inventory may incur additional holding costs, it can prove invaluable in mitigating risks associated with unforeseen disruptions.

5. Demand Forecasting and Flexible Production Plans

Demand forecasting is a critical strategy for reducing supply chain risks, as it helps businesses anticipate fluctuations in demand and adjust their supply chain operations accordingly. By using advanced forecasting techniques and data analytics, companies can predict demand trends more accurately, ensuring that they have the right products and materials on hand.

A flexible production plan is also essential in responding to changes in demand or supply disruptions. Businesses should be prepared to quickly adjust production schedules, reorder raw materials, or even change product offerings based on shifting market conditions. Having a responsive, agile approach to production can help ensure that the business remains operational during times of uncertainty.

6. Technology Integration for Risk Mitigation

Technology plays a pivotal role in enhancing supply chain resilience. Integrating advanced technologies such as Artificial Intelligence (AI), machine learning, and blockchain can help supply chains predict disruptions, streamline operations, and improve decision-making.

AI-powered predictive analytics can be used to forecast potential disruptions, from supplier failures to transport delays, and recommend mitigation strategies. Machine learning algorithms can analyze historical data to detect patterns of supply chain inefficiencies or vulnerabilities and suggest preventive measures.

Blockchain technology, which provides a secure, transparent ledger of transactions, can enhance trust among supply chain partners, enabling them to share data securely and verify the authenticity of goods in real-time. This technology can also improve traceability, helping businesses identify the origins of products and monitor their movement through the supply chain, which is especially crucial in managing risks related to fraud, counterfeiting, or compliance violations.

7. Crisis Management and Business Continuity Plans

A robust crisis management plan is essential for responding to disruptions effectively. This plan should outline the steps the organization will take in the event of a disruption, from immediate actions to long-term recovery strategies. It should also identify key stakeholders, resources, and communication channels necessary to coordinate the response to a crisis.

Business continuity planning (BCP) is an extension of crisis management and involves preparing for the continuation of critical business functions in the event of a significant disruption. BCP includes determining essential operations, securing backup suppliers or service providers, and establishing contingency plans for workforce management, IT systems, and customer communication.

8. Scenario Planning and Stress Testing

Scenario planning and stress testing involve assessing how different types of disruptions could impact the supply chain and developing contingency plans for each scenario. By simulating potential risks, businesses can identify vulnerabilities in their supply chains and test their resilience under various conditions.

Regular stress testing and scenario planning exercises can help businesses prepare for worst-case scenarios, such as supplier bankruptcy, natural disasters, or regulatory changes. These exercises enable companies to understand how their supply chain will perform under stress and refine their risk management strategies.

Building resilient supply chains is not a one-time effort but an ongoing process that requires constant monitoring, adjustment, and improvement. Companies must stay proactive in identifying potential risks, investing in technologies and strategies that enhance flexibility and adaptability, and developing strong relationships with suppliers. Resilience is not just about managing disruptions when they occur but also about building a supply chain that is capable of evolving in response to changes and challenges in the external environment. By adopting these strategies, businesses can ensure that they are prepared to navigate disruptions and continue delivering value to customers, even in the face of uncertainty.

Case Studies on Successful Resilience Practices

The importance of building resilient supply chains has become increasingly evident, especially in light of the recent global disruptions caused by the COVID-19 pandemic, natural disasters, and geopolitical instability. Numerous organizations have adopted innovative strategies to ensure their supply chains are robust and capable of recovering quickly from unforeseen challenges. Below, we explore case studies from leading companies across various industries that have successfully implemented resilience practices, highlighting the strategies they used and the lessons learned.

1. Toyota: Lean Supply Chain Management and Disaster Resilience

Toyota is widely recognized for its lean manufacturing and just-in-time (JIT) production system. This approach minimizes waste and optimizes inventory, ensuring that components and materials are delivered precisely when needed, reducing costs associated with storage and idle inventory. However, Toyota's lean supply chain model was severely tested by the 2011 earthquake and tsunami in Japan, which caused widespread disruptions to its operations.

In response, Toyota implemented a series of resilience practices that helped it recover quickly from the disaster. The company adopted a "supply chain recovery plan" which included improving supplier collaboration and enhancing supply chain visibility. Toyota also invested in dual sourcing for critical components, allowing it to mitigate risks associated with relying on a single supplier or location. Additionally, the company emphasized the importance of supply chain flexibility, enabling quick shifts in production lines to accommodate shortages of parts and materials.

Through these efforts, Toyota was able to resume production faster than many of its competitors, demonstrating the importance of robust contingency planning, supplier diversification, and supply chain transparency. The company's experience underscores the importance of creating an adaptable supply chain that can respond swiftly to disruptions and minimize the impact on overall operations.

2. Apple: Diversification and Global Supplier Network

Apple's global supply chain is one of the most complex and expansive in the world, with components sourced from numerous countries and assembled primarily in China. The company faced a significant challenge during the COVID-19 pandemic, as lockdowns and travel restrictions in China disrupted its manufacturing operations. With factories closed and supply lines severely impacted, Apple needed to ensure that it could continue to meet demand for its products despite these disruptions.

To bolster its resilience, Apple quickly leveraged its diverse supplier network and explored alternative manufacturing locations in countries such as India and Vietnam. This diversification strategy allowed Apple to reduce its dependence on a single region, thus spreading the risk of supply chain disruptions. Moreover, Apple strengthened its relationships with key suppliers by improving communication and sharing real-time data on inventory levels, production schedules, and demand forecasts.

Apple's ability to quickly pivot to new suppliers and manufacturing locations was a critical factor in minimizing the impact of the pandemic on its operations. This case study demonstrates the importance of having a flexible and diversified supply chain that can adapt to sudden changes in the global landscape. It also highlights the value of strong supplier relationships and the role of data-driven decision-making in navigating crises.

3. Unilever: Sustainable Sourcing and Risk Mitigation

Unilever, one of the world's largest consumer goods companies, has long focused on sustainability and risk management as key components of its supply chain strategy. As part of its "Sustainable Living Plan," Unilever has committed to reducing the environmental impact of its supply chain and sourcing raw materials in a way that supports long-term sustainability.

Unilever's resilience strategy emphasizes responsible sourcing and building strong partnerships with suppliers to ensure consistent access to materials. The company has developed a "supply chain resilience index," which helps identify areas of vulnerability in its supply chain, such as reliance on a single supplier or region. This tool allows Unilever to proactively manage risks and build greater resilience into its sourcing strategy.

For example, in response to the risks posed by climate change and natural disasters, Unilever has diversified its sourcing of key agricultural raw materials, such as palm oil and soy, and has implemented programs to help farmers adopt climate-resilient agricultural practices. These efforts not only improve the sustainability of its supply chain but also reduce the risk of disruption from supply shortages caused by environmental factors.

Unilever's focus on sustainable sourcing and risk management has allowed it to build a resilient supply chain that is better equipped to withstand disruptions. This case study illustrates the benefits of integrating sustainability into supply chain resilience practices and the importance of proactive risk identification and mitigation.

4. Amazon: Advanced Technology and Real-Time Data for Resilience

Amazon is a prime example of a company that has leveraged technology to build a resilient supply chain. As the world's largest e-commerce platform, Amazon's supply chain faces constant challenges related to demand fluctuations, logistical complexities, and the need for rapid fulfillment. The company has built resilience by utilizing advanced technologies such as artificial intelligence (AI), machine learning, and robotics, which enable it to quickly respond to disruptions and optimize operations.

One of Amazon's most significant achievements in building resilience is its use of AI and machine learning algorithms to forecast demand and optimize inventory levels. These technologies help Amazon predict shifts in customer behavior, allowing it to adjust its supply chain operations in real time. In addition, Amazon employs a network of fulfillment centers strategically located around the globe, which allows the company to quickly reroute products in case of disruptions, such as transportation delays or warehouse issues.

During the COVID-19 pandemic, Amazon faced an unprecedented surge in demand for essential goods. The company relied on its advanced technology and robust fulfillment network to meet this demand, ensuring timely deliveries even under challenging conditions. Furthermore, Amazon's ability to scale its operations quickly, adapt to fluctuating demand, and maintain operational efficiency demonstrated the effectiveness of integrating advanced technologies into supply chain resilience strategies.

This case study highlights the importance of technology in building supply chain resilience. By investing in automation, data analytics, and real-time visibility, Amazon has created a supply chain that can respond quickly and efficiently to disruptions, ensuring customer satisfaction and maintaining operational continuity.

5. Procter & Gamble (P&G): End-to-End Visibility and Collaborative Networks

Procter & Gamble (P&G), one of the world's largest consumer goods companies, has been a leader in adopting resilient supply chain practices. P&G's supply chain is vast and complex, with thousands of suppliers, manufacturing plants, and distribution centers across the globe. To build resilience, P&G has focused on improving end-to-end visibility and creating collaborative networks with its suppliers and customers.

P&G employs advanced supply chain management systems that provide real-time visibility into its supply chain operations. This enables the company to monitor inventory levels, track shipments, and quickly identify potential disruptions. Furthermore, P&G has developed strong relationships with its suppliers, sharing forecasts, production schedules, and inventory data to improve coordination and responsiveness.

During the COVID-19 pandemic, P&G demonstrated the effectiveness of its resilient supply chain by rapidly adjusting production and distribution plans to meet the surge in demand for cleaning and hygiene products. The company worked closely with suppliers to secure raw materials and maintain production, while simultaneously managing its distribution network to ensure timely delivery to customers.

P&G's success in navigating the pandemic illustrates the importance of visibility and collaboration in building a resilient supply chain. By investing in technology, improving communication with partners, and maintaining flexibility in its operations, P&G has been able to quickly adapt to changing conditions and continue delivering essential products to consumers.

The case studies presented above highlight the diverse strategies that companies across various industries have employed to build resilient supply chains. Key takeaways include the importance of supplier diversification, leveraging technology for real-time data and decision-making, maintaining strong supplier relationships, and developing proactive risk management and contingency plans. Each of these companies has learned valuable lessons from their experiences with disruptions, and their resilience practices provide useful insights for organizations looking to strengthen their own supply chains.

In today's dynamic business environment, resilience is no longer a luxury but a necessity. Companies that invest in building flexible, adaptable, and data-driven supply chains will be better equipped to navigate disruptions, mitigate risks, and maintain operational continuity, regardless of the challenges they may face.

Part 5: Procurement and Supply Chain Leadership

Chapter 14: Leadership in Procurement and Supply Chain

Effective leadership in procurement and supply chain management is critical to driving the success of any organization. In today's dynamic business environment, leaders must possess a broad set of skills that enable them to navigate complex challenges, foster collaboration across departments, and deliver results that align with the organization's strategic goals. This chapter will explore the key skills required for modern procurement and supply chain leaders and highlight the importance of collaboration across teams and departments in achieving business success.

Skills for Modern Procurement and Supply Chain Leaders

The role of procurement and supply chain leaders has evolved significantly over the years. Traditional leadership models focused primarily on cost-cutting and operational efficiency. While these remain important objectives, modern supply chain leaders are required to balance multiple priorities, such as risk management, sustainability, innovation, and customer satisfaction. To excel in this environment, leaders must develop a diverse skill set that enables them to manage both strategic and operational challenges effectively.

1. Strategic Thinking and Decision-Making

One of the most crucial skills for supply chain and procurement leaders is the ability to think strategically. A leader must understand the broader goals of the business and align procurement and supply chain strategies with these objectives. This includes identifying new opportunities for cost reduction, improving supplier relationships, and ensuring that the supply chain is agile and resilient in the face of market changes.

Strategic thinking also involves assessing long-term trends, such as shifts in global trade, technological innovations, and regulatory changes, and preparing the supply chain to adapt to these factors. Effective decision-making is a core component of strategic leadership, as it allows leaders to make informed choices that balance short-term needs with long-term goals.

2. Financial Acumen

Procurement and supply chain leaders must possess strong financial skills to effectively manage budgets, negotiate contracts, and assess the total cost of ownership (TCO) for procurement decisions. Understanding financial concepts, such as cost-benefit analysis, return on investment (ROI), and total cost analysis, allows leaders to make decisions that support the financial health of the organization.

Leaders with financial acumen can also identify opportunities to reduce costs and improve profitability while ensuring that the supply chain remains efficient and effective. A focus on cost control and resource optimization, combined with a deep understanding of financial metrics, is essential for modern supply chain leaders to navigate economic uncertainties and drive sustainable growth.

3. Technology and Data-Driven Decision-Making

Technology has become an integral part of supply chain management, and leaders must be comfortable using advanced tools and systems to drive efficiency and innovation. Familiarity with enterprise resource planning (ERP) systems, supply chain management software, and data analytics platforms is essential for modern supply chain leadership.

Data-driven decision-making is an increasingly important skill for leaders in this field. The ability to collect, analyze, and interpret data enables leaders to make informed decisions that improve supply chain performance. For example, leaders can use predictive analytics to forecast demand, optimize inventory levels, and improve supplier performance. They can also use data to assess risks and identify opportunities for continuous improvement.

4. Negotiation and Relationship Management

Procurement and supply chain leaders are often required to negotiate with suppliers, vendors, and other stakeholders. Strong negotiation skills are essential for securing favorable terms, pricing, and delivery schedules. Successful negotiators understand the needs and interests of all parties involved and work to find mutually beneficial solutions.

Building and maintaining strong relationships with suppliers and other external partners is equally important. Procurement and supply chain leaders must foster collaboration, transparency, and trust in these relationships. Effective relationship management enables leaders to secure high-quality products and services, reduce lead times, and mitigate risks associated with supply chain disruptions.

5. Risk Management and Resilience Building

The ability to identify and manage risks is one of the most important skills for supply chain leaders in today's volatile environment. Leaders must be able to assess potential risks in areas such as supplier performance, geopolitical instability, natural disasters, and supply chain disruptions. Once risks are identified, leaders need to develop strategies to mitigate them, whether through supplier diversification, contingency planning, or the use of technology to enhance supply chain visibility.

Building resilience in the supply chain is also a critical responsibility of procurement and supply chain leaders. A resilient supply chain can quickly adapt to changes and recover from disruptions, ensuring that the organization continues to meet customer demands and maintain operational efficiency.

6. Communication and Influencing Skills

Effective communication is key to successful leadership in procurement and supply chain management. Leaders must be able to communicate clearly with internal stakeholders, such as senior management, cross-functional teams, and employees, as well as with external partners, such as suppliers and logistics providers. Strong communication skills ensure that everyone is aligned on goals, expectations, and performance standards.

Leaders must also possess the ability to influence others. Whether persuading stakeholders to invest in new technologies, negotiating favorable contracts with suppliers, or driving change within the organization, effective influencing is crucial for driving results. Leaders who can inspire and motivate others to embrace new ideas, processes, and initiatives are better equipped to achieve long-term success.

7. Sustainability and Ethical Leadership

As sustainability becomes an increasingly important focus for businesses, procurement and supply chain leaders must have a strong understanding of sustainable practices and ethical considerations in supply chain management. Leaders must ensure that procurement decisions are aligned with the company's sustainability goals and that suppliers adhere to ethical standards related to labor practices, environmental impact, and corporate social responsibility (CSR).

Ethical leadership also involves making decisions that balance profit with social and environmental considerations. For example, leaders may prioritize sourcing materials from suppliers that use eco-friendly processes or invest in technologies that reduce carbon emissions. Emphasizing sustainability can help companies enhance their brand reputation, reduce operational risks, and contribute to long-term societal well-being.

Collaboration Across Teams and Departments

In today's interconnected business environment, collaboration across teams and departments is essential for success in procurement and supply chain management. Procurement and supply chain leaders must work closely with other functional areas within the organization, such as finance, operations, marketing, and IT, to ensure that supply chain activities align with the organization's overall strategy.

1. Cross-Functional Collaboration

Effective collaboration with other departments is essential for optimizing procurement and supply chain operations. For example, procurement leaders must work closely with the finance team to establish budgets and financial targets, as well as with the operations team to ensure that the right materials and resources are available for production. Similarly, marketing teams rely on supply chain leaders to ensure that products are delivered on time to meet customer demand and that inventory levels are optimized to support promotional activities.

Cross-functional collaboration enables supply chain leaders to understand the needs and challenges of different departments, allowing them to make more informed decisions and drive business outcomes. For example, procurement teams that work closely with the operations department can better anticipate production needs and secure the right materials in a timely manner.

2. Supplier Collaboration and Partnership

In addition to internal collaboration, procurement and supply chain leaders must also collaborate closely with suppliers. Building long-term, strategic partnerships with key suppliers can help organizations secure favorable terms, improve product quality, and reduce lead times. Supplier collaboration is especially important in industries where innovation and technological advancements are crucial for staying competitive.

Strong supplier relationships enable organizations to share information, such as forecasts, production schedules, and inventory levels, to improve coordination and reduce inefficiencies. By fostering open communication and transparency, procurement leaders can ensure that suppliers are aligned with the organization's goals and are better able to respond to changing demands or disruptions in the supply chain.

3. Collaboration with Customers

Collaboration with customers is another critical aspect of modern procurement and supply chain leadership. Understanding customer needs and preferences allows procurement leaders to ensure that products and services meet the desired specifications and are delivered on time. Close collaboration with customers also enables supply chain leaders to anticipate demand fluctuations, manage inventory levels effectively, and develop strategies for continuous improvement.

Supply chain leaders must also consider the customer experience when making decisions about sourcing, production, and logistics. By integrating customer feedback into the supply chain process, procurement and supply chain leaders can improve customer satisfaction, reduce costs, and enhance brand loyalty.

Leadership in procurement and supply chain management is a multifaceted role that requires a diverse skill set and the ability to collaborate across teams and departments. Modern supply chain leaders must be strategic thinkers, financial stewards, technology-savvy decision-makers, and effective communicators. By fostering collaboration within the organization and with external partners, leaders can ensure that the supply chain operates efficiently, mitigates risks, and aligns with the organization's broader objectives.

The role of supply chain leadership has become more complex and challenging in today's globalized and rapidly changing business environment. However, by developing the necessary skills and embracing a collaborative, data-driven approach, procurement and supply chain leaders can navigate these challenges and drive long-term success for their organizations.

Leadership Case Studies in Procurement and Supply Chain Management

Leadership in procurement and supply chain management plays a pivotal role in driving the strategic objectives of an organization.

Successful leaders in these fields navigate complex challenges, adapt to evolving markets, and inspire their teams to deliver exceptional results. In this section, we will examine case studies of effective leadership in procurement and supply chain management, illustrating how visionary leadership has led to transformative changes, enhanced operational efficiency, and the creation of resilient, sustainable supply chains.

Case Study 1: Apple Inc. - Transforming Supply Chain Leadership for Competitive Advantage

Apple Inc. is one of the most well-known global companies, renowned not only for its innovative products but also for its highly effective supply chain management. Apple's supply chain is widely regarded as one of the most efficient and sophisticated in the world. The leadership behind Apple's supply chain, particularly under the stewardship of former Chief Operating Officer Tim Cook, has been critical in transforming the company's global supply chain into a competitive advantage.

Tim Cook's Leadership in Supply Chain Optimization

Tim Cook's leadership style in supply chain management focused on several key strategies that helped Apple build its supply chain into a model of efficiency and reliability. Under his leadership, Apple focused on long-term supplier relationships, implementing tight control over its inventory, and a commitment to precision and consistency in production. One of Cook's key leadership decisions was to maintain strict control over the entire supply chain, from the sourcing of raw materials to the distribution of finished products. This control ensured that Apple could minimize risk, maintain product quality, and maximize profit margins.

Cook's leadership also emphasized strategic supplier partnerships, which allowed Apple to negotiate favorable terms and secure exclusive access to key components. For instance, Apple negotiated long-term contracts with suppliers like Foxconn, ensuring a steady and reliable supply of critical components, such as chips and displays. This long-term commitment gave Apple a competitive edge by reducing supplier bargaining power and ensuring that the company could meet the ever-growing demand for its products.

Innovation and Technology Integration

Under Tim Cook's leadership, Apple also became a pioneer in the integration of technology into supply chain management. The company was one of the first to implement RFID and GPS tracking to improve visibility across its global supply chain. By leveraging real-time data, Apple could track shipments and monitor inventory levels with a level of accuracy and efficiency that few companies could match.

Additionally, Apple's focus on innovation extended beyond product development to include supply chain processes. For example, Apple optimized its logistics operations by consolidating shipping and creating direct-to-consumer delivery systems, which helped reduce shipping times and costs.

Impact of Leadership

Cook's leadership was instrumental in Apple's ability to maintain market leadership in the face of rapidly changing consumer preferences, global competition, and economic volatility. Apple's supply chain was able to deliver products on time, with minimal inventory and at scale, enabling the company to maintain high profitability. Today, Apple's supply chain remains a key element of its success, and its leadership approach continues to serve as a benchmark for excellence in procurement and supply chain management.

Case Study 2: Unilever - Leadership in Sustainability and Ethical Sourcing

Unilever, a global leader in consumer goods, has made sustainability a cornerstone of its supply chain strategy. With the appointment of leaders like Paul Polman, former CEO, the company has undergone a major transformation, aligning its supply chain practices with environmental and social governance (ESG) objectives.

Paul Polman's Vision for Sustainable Leadership

Under the leadership of Paul Polman, Unilever took bold steps to integrate sustainability into its core supply chain operations. Polman's vision was to move beyond short-term profit maximization and focus on long-term value creation through sustainable business practices. His leadership was pivotal in aligning Unilever's procurement and supply chain activities with the company's broader sustainability agenda, focusing on reducing environmental impact, promoting ethical sourcing, and ensuring fair labor practices across the supply chain.

Polman was a key advocate for Unilever's Sustainable Living Plan, which set ambitious targets to reduce the company's carbon footprint, improve water usage, and enhance the social and environmental impact of its supply chain. For example, Unilever focused on reducing its environmental footprint by sourcing sustainable raw materials such as palm oil, soy, and paper, while also striving to eliminate deforestation from its supply chain.

Supplier Collaboration and Ethical Sourcing

One of the core strategies under Polman's leadership was supplier collaboration. Unilever recognized that it could not achieve its sustainability goals in isolation and needed to work closely with suppliers to drive change across the supply chain. This included implementing a "sustainable sourcing" approach, where Unilever worked with farmers, suppliers, and manufacturers to promote sustainable agricultural practices, such as reducing pesticide use and improving soil health.

Unilever also focused on developing long-term relationships with its suppliers, ensuring that they adhered to the company's ethical sourcing standards. The company invested in initiatives that helped suppliers improve labor conditions and ensure fair wages, promoting ethical sourcing practices across its entire supply chain.

Impact of Leadership

Polman's leadership has had a profound impact on Unilever's business performance, as the company has become a recognized leader in sustainability within the consumer goods industry. Under his leadership, Unilever's supply chain became a key driver of innovation, with sustainability initiatives helping to reduce costs, mitigate risks, and enhance brand reputation. Additionally, Unilever's focus on sustainability has led to increased consumer loyalty, as more customers prioritize ethical sourcing and environmental stewardship in their purchasing decisions.

Today, Unilever's commitment to sustainability continues to guide its procurement and supply chain practices, setting a high standard for other organizations seeking to align business operations with broader social and environmental goals.

Case Study 3: Walmart - Leadership in Supply Chain Integration and Cost Leadership

Walmart, the world's largest retailer, has long been a leader in supply chain management. The company's leadership in supply chain innovation, driven by figures such as former CEO Lee Scott, has helped Walmart maintain its competitive edge in the highly competitive retail sector. Walmart's leadership in supply chain management is rooted in its ability to integrate technology, foster supplier collaboration, and maintain its commitment to cost leadership.

Lee Scott's Leadership in Supply Chain Efficiency

Under Lee Scott's leadership, Walmart revolutionized its supply chain by focusing on operational efficiency, cost-cutting, and supply chain integration. One of Scott's major contributions was his focus on streamlining Walmart's supply chain through the integration of advanced technology, including barcode scanning and real-time inventory tracking. This technology enabled Walmart to optimize its distribution and inventory management processes, ensuring that products were always available to customers without overstocking.

Scott also recognized the importance of supplier collaboration in achieving cost leadership. Walmart established long-term partnerships with key suppliers, negotiating favorable terms and implementing a Vendor-Managed Inventory (VMI) system that allowed suppliers to monitor inventory levels and manage product replenishment. This collaboration helped reduce costs and improve product availability while ensuring that Walmart could pass savings onto customers.

Global Supply Chain Integration

Walmart's leadership also extended to its global supply chain operations. As the company expanded into international markets, it faced new challenges related to logistics, customs, and inventory management. However, Walmart's leadership in supply chain integration helped the company build a seamless global network, enabling it to source products from low-cost regions while maintaining high standards of operational efficiency.

In addition to integrating supply chain technology, Walmart also leveraged its scale to negotiate lower prices from suppliers, ensuring that the company remained competitive in the marketplace. By focusing on cost control and efficient operations, Walmart has maintained its position as the low-cost leader in the retail industry.

Impact of Leadership

Lee Scott's leadership has had a lasting impact on Walmart's ability to maintain its position as the world's largest retailer. Under his leadership, Walmart's supply chain became a critical competitive advantage, allowing the company to provide low prices and a wide product assortment to customers. The company's focus on supply chain integration and cost leadership has enabled it to maintain profitability while delivering value to customers, reinforcing its status as a leader in retail.

Case Study 4: Nike - Leadership in Innovation and Resilient Supply Chains

Nike, one of the world's leading sportswear companies, has faced numerous challenges in its supply chain, including rising labor costs, supply chain disruptions, and increasing demand for sustainable products. Under the leadership of CEO Mark Parker, Nike has made significant strides in leveraging technology, fostering innovation, and building a more resilient and sustainable supply chain.

Mark Parker's Leadership in Supply Chain Innovation

Mark Parker's leadership emphasized the importance of innovation in both products and supply chain processes. Nike's supply chain management has been shaped by a commitment to agility, with the company focusing on leveraging technology and data analytics to optimize inventory management, production, and distribution. Nike introduced advanced analytics tools and artificial intelligence (AI) to improve demand forecasting and inventory management, ensuring that products were delivered to the right locations at the right time.

Parker also pushed Nike toward building a more resilient supply chain by diversifying suppliers and sourcing materials from a broader range of regions. This diversification helped reduce Nike's dependence on any single supplier or region, mitigating risks associated with supply chain disruptions, such as natural disasters, political instability, or economic downturns.

Sustainability and Ethical Sourcing

Under Parker's leadership, Nike also made significant strides in sustainable sourcing. Nike has implemented various initiatives to reduce the environmental impact of its supply chain, including using recycled materials in products and reducing carbon emissions in production processes. Nike also focused on improving labor practices across its supply chain by working with suppliers to ensure fair wages and safe working conditions.

Nike's leadership in sustainability has helped the company meet growing consumer demand for eco-friendly products while enhancing brand loyalty. Through innovative practices and a commitment to sustainability, Nike has not only optimized its supply chain but also positioned itself as a responsible corporate citizen in the global marketplace.

Impact of Leadership

Mark Parker's leadership has been instrumental in helping Nike maintain its competitive edge in the sportswear industry. By leveraging technology, fostering innovation, and focusing on sustainability, Nike has built a resilient and efficient supply chain that can adapt to changing market conditions and consumer preferences. Nike's supply chain leadership continues to serve as a model for companies seeking to balance profitability, innovation, and sustainability.

These case studies highlight the critical role that leadership plays in driving innovation, sustainability, and operational efficiency within procurement and supply chain management. The leaders of Apple, Unilever, Walmart, and Nike have demonstrated how strategic decision-making, collaboration with suppliers, and a focus on technology can transform supply chain operations. By examining these leadership strategies, companies can gain valuable insights into building more resilient, efficient, and sustainable supply chains.

Chapter 15: Performance Measurement

Performance measurement in procurement and supply chain management is essential for ensuring that organizations are operating efficiently, meeting their strategic objectives, and delivering value to stakeholders. The ability to measure performance accurately is crucial for identifying areas for improvement, optimizing operations, and maintaining competitive advantage. Two of the most commonly used tools in this regard are Key Performance Indicators (KPIs) and the Balanced Scorecard approach. These tools enable organizations to assess various aspects of their supply chain and procurement functions, ensuring alignment with broader business goals.

Key Performance Indicators (KPIs) for Procurement and Supply Chain

KPIs are quantifiable metrics that organizations use to gauge the performance of their procurement and supply chain activities. These indicators provide insight into the efficiency, effectiveness, and overall health of the supply chain, helping decision-makers identify strengths, weaknesses, and areas for improvement. The selection of relevant KPIs is crucial as it ensures that organizations track the right aspects of their operations, which ultimately supports decision-making and performance optimization.

1. Cost-Related KPIs

Cost management is a core aspect of procurement and supply chain performance, and KPIs in this area focus on controlling and reducing costs while maximizing value. Some important cost-related KPIs include:

> **Cost of Goods Sold (COGS):** This KPI tracks the total direct costs associated with the production of goods sold by a company, including materials, labor, and overhead costs. Monitoring COGS helps organizations assess the effectiveness of their procurement strategies and cost control measures.

Procurement Cost Savings: This metric evaluates the savings achieved through effective sourcing strategies, vendor negotiations, and supply chain optimization. It is a key indicator of procurement performance and supplier relationship management.

Total Cost of Ownership (TCO): TCO measures the complete cost associated with acquiring and maintaining a product or service, including purchase price, maintenance, and operational costs. It provides a more holistic view of procurement costs and allows businesses to make better long-term purchasing decisions.

2. Quality-Related KPIs

Quality is a critical component of both procurement and supply chain management. High-quality standards ensure customer satisfaction, minimize waste, and reduce returns and rework costs. Relevant KPIs include:

Supplier Quality Performance: This KPI measures the quality of products or services delivered by suppliers. Metrics such as defect rates, returns, and product compliance help organizations monitor the effectiveness of their supplier selection and management processes.

On-Time Delivery (OTD): On-time delivery is a critical performance measure that ensures products and materials arrive as scheduled. Delays can disrupt production schedules and affect customer satisfaction, so monitoring this KPI is essential for evaluating supplier reliability and logistics performance.

Inventory Quality: This metric tracks the quality of inventory in terms of spoilage, damage, or obsolescence. It is an important KPI for managing inventory turnover and ensuring that inventory remains in good condition for distribution or production use.

3. Efficiency-Related KPIs

Efficiency KPIs focus on the optimization of processes, resource utilization, and operational performance across the procurement and supply chain functions. Key efficiency metrics include:

> **Inventory Turnover:** This KPI measures how quickly inventory is sold and replaced over a period. High inventory turnover indicates efficient inventory management, while low turnover can signal excess stock and potential obsolescence.

> **Order Cycle Time:** The order cycle time tracks the total time from order placement to delivery. Shorter cycle times reflect efficient order processing and logistics management, while longer cycle times may highlight inefficiencies in the supply chain.

> **Fill Rate:** This KPI measures the percentage of customer orders that are fulfilled from existing stock without backorders. A high fill rate indicates an efficient supply chain that can meet demand without delay.

4. Customer-Related KPIs

Customer satisfaction is paramount in procurement and supply chain management, as it directly impacts revenue and brand loyalty. Customer-related KPIs include:

> **Customer Satisfaction (CSAT):** This KPI tracks customer satisfaction with products and services delivered through the supply chain. High CSAT scores indicate that the supply chain is effectively meeting customer expectations in terms of product quality and delivery performance.

Perfect Order Rate: The perfect order rate measures the percentage of orders delivered to customers without any issues, including damage, late delivery, or incorrect products. Achieving a high perfect order rate is a sign of operational excellence and strong supplier relationships.

Balanced Scorecard Approach

The Balanced Scorecard (BSC) is a strategic performance management framework that helps organizations measure and align their activities with their long-term objectives. Unlike traditional financial performance metrics, which focus primarily on short-term results, the BSC takes a more comprehensive approach by considering multiple perspectives. It helps organizations monitor key drivers of performance, align activities with strategic goals, and create a balanced view of success across different areas of the business.

Developed by Robert Kaplan and David Norton in the early 1990s, the BSC includes four main perspectives: Financial, Customer, Internal Processes, and Learning & Growth. By evaluating performance across these dimensions, organizations gain a more holistic view of their supply chain and procurement operations.

1. Financial Perspective

The financial perspective of the Balanced Scorecard focuses on the financial outcomes of supply chain and procurement activities. It includes traditional financial KPIs that measure profitability, cost efficiency, and revenue growth. This perspective helps organizations assess how their procurement and supply chain decisions impact the bottom line. Some relevant financial KPIs include:

Cost Savings and Cost Control: The financial impact of cost-saving initiatives, procurement strategies, and supplier negotiations. These KPIs measure how well the organization controls costs while delivering value.

Return on Assets (ROA): This metric evaluates the return generated on the company's assets, including inventory and supply chain investments.

Cash Flow: Effective management of cash flow is crucial for procurement and supply chain management. This KPI measures how well working capital is managed, including inventory and receivables, and how it impacts the company's liquidity.

2. Customer Perspective

The customer perspective measures how well procurement and supply chain activities satisfy customer needs and expectations. Key performance indicators in this category evaluate the company's ability to deliver value to customers, enhance satisfaction, and maintain loyalty. Important KPIs include:

Customer Satisfaction (CSAT) and Net Promoter Score (NPS): These metrics measure customer perceptions of the company's products, services, and delivery performance. High customer satisfaction indicates that the procurement and supply chain functions are effectively meeting customer demands.

On-Time Delivery and Lead Time: These KPIs assess the company's ability to meet customer delivery expectations, a key factor in maintaining customer loyalty and satisfaction.

Customer Retention Rate: This metric tracks the percentage of customers retained over a specified period. High retention rates suggest that the supply chain is successfully delivering value and maintaining strong relationships with customers.

3. Internal Processes Perspective

The internal processes perspective evaluates the efficiency and effectiveness of key supply chain and procurement processes. This includes optimizing workflows, reducing waste, improving cycle times, and increasing process agility. Key internal process KPIs include:

> **Cycle Time Efficiency:** This KPI evaluates the efficiency of order fulfillment, procurement lead times, and product delivery timelines. Shorter cycle times indicate an agile and responsive supply chain.
>
> **Process Compliance and Standardization:** This KPI measures adherence to established procurement and supply chain processes. Consistent process execution ensures reliability and minimizes risk.
>
> **Innovation and Continuous Improvement:** Metrics that track the company's efforts to innovate and improve procurement and supply chain processes, such as the implementation of new technologies or process redesigns.

4. Learning & Growth Perspective

The learning and growth perspective focuses on the ability of the organization to innovate, develop its workforce, and foster a culture of continuous improvement. KPIs in this category assess the effectiveness of training, development, and knowledge-sharing initiatives. Key KPIs include:

> **Employee Training and Development:** This KPI tracks the number of hours spent on employee training, professional development, and skill-building activities.
>
> **Employee Satisfaction and Retention:** High employee satisfaction levels are a strong indicator of a healthy, motivated

workforce. Retaining skilled employees ensures continuity and expertise within procurement and supply chain functions.

Technology Adoption and Innovation: This KPI measures the extent to which new technologies, tools, or systems are adopted to improve procurement and supply chain operations, enabling the company to stay competitive.

Conclusion

Performance measurement is essential for driving success in procurement and supply chain management. By utilizing KPIs and the Balanced Scorecard approach, organizations can gain comprehensive insights into their operations and align their activities with their strategic objectives. KPIs provide actionable data to evaluate cost efficiency, quality, customer satisfaction, and operational efficiency, while the Balanced Scorecard offers a holistic framework for monitoring performance across financial, customer, internal, and learning perspectives. Together, these tools enable organizations to optimize their supply chains, enhance decision-making, and ultimately create sustainable value for all stakeholders.

Continuous improvement frameworks.

Continuous improvement is a core principle in both procurement and supply chain management, as it enables organizations to enhance efficiency, reduce waste, improve product quality, and maintain competitiveness in a rapidly changing market. To achieve continuous improvement, businesses need structured frameworks that guide and support their improvement efforts over time. These frameworks provide a systematic approach to identifying problems, developing solutions, implementing changes, and measuring results. A variety of continuous improvement frameworks are utilized across different industries, each with its own focus and methodology. Below are some of the most widely adopted frameworks in procurement and supply chain management.

1. Lean Management Framework

The Lean management framework is rooted in the Toyota Production System (TPS) and focuses on eliminating waste and enhancing value for customers. The core concept of Lean is to create more value with fewer resources by identifying and eliminating activities that do not add value to the customer. In procurement and supply chain management, Lean principles can be applied to streamline processes, reduce lead times, lower costs, and improve overall performance.

Key Lean Principles:

> **Value Stream Mapping:** This tool helps businesses map out their entire supply chain, identifying each step and evaluating whether it adds value. Non-value-adding activities (waste) are then eliminated to streamline the process.
>
> **Just-in-Time (JIT):** This principle focuses on producing or delivering goods only when they are needed, thus reducing inventory costs and minimizing waste.
>
> **Kaizen (Continuous Improvement):** Kaizen is a key component of Lean, emphasizing small, incremental improvements on a daily basis. The goal is to foster a culture where everyone in the organization contributes to finding solutions to inefficiencies and problems.
>
> **5S:** This method helps create a clean, organized, and efficient work environment. The 5S steps—Sort, Set in Order, Shine, Standardize, and Sustain—help organizations improve efficiency, safety, and productivity in their operations.

Impact on Procurement and Supply Chain:

In procurement, Lean principles can lead to better supplier relationships, lower inventory levels, and faster order fulfillment times. In supply chain management, Lean helps reduce waste across the entire value chain, making it easier to manage costs, improve service levels, and optimize resource usage.

2. Six Sigma Framework

Six Sigma is a data-driven methodology aimed at improving the quality of processes by identifying and removing the causes of defects and variability. The framework, developed by Motorola in the 1980s, focuses on achieving process excellence by reducing defects to a rate of 3.4 defects per million opportunities. In procurement and supply chain management, Six Sigma techniques are used to optimize processes, enhance product quality, and minimize costs by focusing on process improvements through statistical analysis.

Key Six Sigma Concepts:

> **DMAIC (Define, Measure, Analyze, Improve, Control):** DMAIC is the primary methodology used in Six Sigma. It is a structured, five-step approach that helps identify problems, measure performance, analyze root causes, implement improvements, and control the new processes to maintain improvements over time.
>
> **Statistical Process Control (SPC):** SPC is used to monitor and control processes by using data to detect variations and prevent defects from occurring. It involves using control charts to track performance over time.
>
> **Defect Reduction:** Six Sigma focuses on reducing variability and eliminating defects in processes, which directly impacts quality. By identifying and removing sources of variability, organizations can consistently meet customer expectations.

Impact on Procurement and Supply Chain:

In procurement, Six Sigma can be used to improve supplier performance, reduce the frequency of defects in materials, and enhance procurement efficiency. In supply chain management, Six Sigma can reduce variability in lead times, enhance product quality, and reduce costs through improved process control and defect reduction.

3. Total Quality Management (TQM) Framework

Total Quality Management (TQM) is an organization-wide approach to improving the quality of products, services, and processes. The goal of TQM is to embed quality into every aspect of an organization's operations by involving all employees in the continuous improvement process. TQM emphasizes customer satisfaction, employee involvement, and data-driven decision-making to improve quality.

Key TQM Principles:

> **Customer Focus:** The primary goal of TQM is to meet or exceed customer expectations. By focusing on customer needs and feedback, organizations can continuously improve their products and services.
>
> **Employee Involvement:** TQM encourages the active involvement of employees at all levels in the improvement process. Employees are seen as valuable contributors to identifying problems and generating solutions.
>
> **Process Approach:** TQM emphasizes the importance of processes and systems. By improving the processes that contribute to quality, organizations can reduce variability and achieve consistency in their outputs.
>
> **Continuous Improvement:** Like Lean, TQM emphasizes the ongoing nature of improvement. It is not seen as a one-time effort but as an ongoing commitment to making incremental improvements over time.

Impact on Procurement and Supply Chain:

TQM can enhance supplier selection and relationship management by ensuring that suppliers meet high-quality standards. It also helps organizations in procurement by fostering an environment of continuous improvement and collaboration. In the broader supply chain, TQM drives process improvements that reduce defects, improve on-time delivery, and enhance customer satisfaction.

4. Theory of Constraints (TOC)

The Theory of Constraints (TOC), developed by Eliyahu Goldratt in the 1980s, is a methodology for identifying the most significant constraint or bottleneck in a system and improving it. The central idea behind TOC is that any system—whether it's a manufacturing process or a supply chain—will have a limiting factor that constrains its overall performance. By focusing improvement efforts on this constraint, organizations can achieve significant improvements in their operations.

Key TOC Concepts:

Identify the Constraint: The first step in TOC is identifying the limiting factor in a process or system. This could be anything from a bottleneck in production to delays in transportation or inventory management.

Exploit the Constraint: Once the constraint is identified, the next step is to exploit it by maximizing its capacity. This may involve prioritizing work that flows through the bottleneck or reducing downtime.

Subordinate Everything Else to the Constraint: All other processes should be aligned to support the constraint. For example, if a particular machine is the bottleneck, the focus should be on ensuring that other processes feed into it efficiently without causing delays.

Elevate the Constraint: If the constraint cannot be adequately addressed through exploitation and subordination, it may be necessary to invest in additional resources or capacity to elevate the constraint.

Repeat the Process: Once a constraint is resolved, the next limiting factor will emerge. The process of identifying and addressing constraints is ongoing and requires continual improvement.

Impact on Procurement and Supply Chain:

TOC can be particularly effective in supply chain management by identifying and alleviating bottlenecks in inventory, production, or distribution. In procurement, TOC helps optimize supplier lead times and reduce delays in the procurement process by identifying the areas where constraints occur most frequently.

5. Kaizen Framework

Kaizen, which means "continuous improvement" in Japanese, is a philosophy that encourages small, incremental improvements on a daily basis. It is widely used in Lean and Six Sigma methodologies but is also valuable as a standalone framework. The goal of Kaizen is to create a culture of continuous improvement, where employees at all levels of the organization are empowered to suggest and implement improvements.

Key Kaizen Concepts:

Small, Incremental Improvements: Unlike other frameworks that may focus on large, transformational changes, Kaizen emphasizes small, continuous improvements that add up over time.

Employee Involvement: Kaizen encourages the active participation of employees in the improvement process. It recognizes that the people closest to the work often have the best ideas for improvement.

Standardization: As improvements are made, the new best practices are standardized to ensure they are consistently applied and maintained.

Waste Elimination: Kaizen, like Lean, focuses on eliminating waste in all forms, including time, materials, and labor.

Impact on Procurement and Supply Chain:

In procurement, Kaizen encourages the ongoing improvement of supplier relationships, contract management processes, and purchasing efficiency. In the supply chain, Kaizen fosters a culture of constant process refinement, leading to better inventory management, optimized distribution, and improved customer satisfaction.

Continuous improvement frameworks play a vital role in optimizing procurement and supply chain operations. Lean management, Six Sigma, TQM, the Theory of Constraints, and Kaizen all provide unique approaches for identifying inefficiencies, addressing problems, and enhancing overall performance. By applying these frameworks, organizations can drive sustainable improvements, enhance customer satisfaction, and create a competitive advantage in the marketplace. The key to success lies in selecting the right framework based on the specific needs and challenges of the organization and committing to continuous, incremental improvements over time.

Chapter 16: Future Trends in Procurement and Supply Chain Management

The Rise of Automation and Autonomous Systems

The future of procurement and supply chain management is being shaped by the rapid rise of automation and autonomous systems, which are driving significant transformation in how businesses operate. As technology advances, organizations are increasingly adopting automation to streamline their processes, improve accuracy, reduce costs, and enhance efficiency. Automation in procurement and supply chains covers a broad range of applications, from robotic process automation (RPA) in back-office functions to autonomous vehicles in transportation and warehousing. These advancements are helping organizations achieve greater operational flexibility, reduce human error, and improve their responsiveness to market demands.

Automation in procurement begins with the digitization of procurement tasks, such as invoice processing, order management, and supplier communication. By using software to automate routine and repetitive tasks, businesses can free up their procurement teams to focus on more strategic functions, such as supplier relationship management and contract negotiation. For example, intelligent procurement systems can automatically match purchase orders with invoices and payments, reducing administrative overhead and the risk of errors. Furthermore, machine learning algorithms can be employed to predict future purchasing needs based on historical data, allowing procurement teams to optimize inventory levels and supplier orders without manual intervention.

In supply chain management, the integration of autonomous systems is revolutionizing logistics and warehousing. Automated Guided Vehicles (AGVs) and drones are increasingly being used in warehouses to move goods, reduce labor costs, and improve operational efficiency. These systems can work around the clock, minimizing downtime and accelerating throughput. Autonomous trucks and delivery vehicles are also becoming more common in the transportation industry, improving the speed and efficiency of last-mile delivery while reducing human dependency and enhancing safety.

The use of artificial intelligence (AI) and machine learning in automation further extends to demand forecasting, route optimization, and supply chain visibility. AI-driven algorithms can analyze large datasets in real-time to provide accurate demand predictions, helping organizations optimize inventory levels and avoid overstocking or stockouts. AI is also used for optimizing routes for delivery trucks, ensuring faster deliveries and reducing transportation costs. Additionally, autonomous systems can be integrated with Internet of Things (IoT) sensors to provide real-time tracking of goods, offering full transparency across the supply chain. This level of visibility enhances decision-making, improves coordination between supply chain partners, and helps mitigate disruptions.

In procurement, the automation of supplier performance monitoring and contract compliance is becoming increasingly important. By using intelligent systems that continuously track supplier performance against agreed-upon metrics, organizations can proactively address issues and ensure that they maintain high levels of supplier performance. Automation in procurement and supply chain management also extends to the area of contract management, where AI-powered tools can automatically review contracts, extract key data, and ensure compliance with terms.

However, while automation presents substantial benefits, it also comes with challenges. Businesses must ensure that they integrate new technologies into their existing systems seamlessly, and they need to invest in the skills and training of their workforce to manage and maintain automated systems. Furthermore, issues related to cybersecurity, data privacy, and system reliability must be addressed to ensure the secure operation of these automated systems.

The future of procurement and supply chain management will undoubtedly see continued advancements in automation and autonomous systems, enabling organizations to streamline operations, enhance customer service, and gain a competitive edge. By embracing these technologies, businesses can reduce costs, improve productivity, and stay ahead in an increasingly fast-paced and complex global marketplace.

Evolving Global Trade Dynamics

Global trade dynamics are undergoing profound changes, driven by shifting political, economic, and technological factors. These changes are reshaping procurement and supply chain management strategies, as organizations must adapt to new trade regulations, market conditions, and geopolitical tensions. In particular, the rise of protectionism, the shift toward regional trade agreements, and the impact of global trade disruptions are creating both challenges and opportunities for supply chain professionals.

One of the most significant shifts in global trade is the move toward regionalization and localization. As trade barriers rise and countries adopt more protectionist policies, companies are increasingly looking to regional supply chains to mitigate risks associated with global trade. Regional trade agreements, such as the Comprehensive and Progressive Agreement for Trans-Pacific Partnership (CPTPP) and the United States-Mexico-Canada Agreement (USMCA), are fostering closer economic ties between neighboring countries, reducing tariffs, and streamlining cross-border trade. By sourcing materials and products from regional suppliers, companies can reduce lead times, lower transportation costs, and decrease exposure to trade disruptions caused by geopolitical events.

At the same time, the ongoing shift towards localization is influencing procurement strategies. Companies are reassessing their global supply chain models and considering the benefits of closer, more resilient relationships with local suppliers. Local sourcing can help mitigate risks associated with long supply chains, such as delays due to transportation bottlenecks, geopolitical tensions, or natural disasters. It also enables organizations to respond more quickly to customer demands and reduce their carbon footprint by minimizing the distance goods need to travel.

The global trade landscape is also influenced by the rise of digital trade, which is transforming how goods and services are exchanged across borders. E-commerce platforms, digital payment systems, and blockchain technology are enabling businesses to engage in cross-border trade more easily and securely. Blockchain, in particular, is being used to enhance transparency and traceability in global supply chains. By providing an immutable, decentralized record of transactions, blockchain ensures that businesses can verify the authenticity of products, track their movement across the supply chain, and ensure compliance with international trade regulations.

Geopolitical tensions and trade wars are also significantly shaping global trade dynamics. For example, the trade dispute between the United States and China has led many organizations to rethink their supply chain strategies, particularly regarding reliance on Chinese suppliers. The imposition of tariffs and trade restrictions has prompted some companies to shift their production to other low-cost countries, such as Vietnam, India, or Mexico, to maintain cost competitiveness. These trade tensions have also highlighted the need for businesses to have more flexible, diversified supply chains that can quickly adapt to changing trade policies.

Brexit is another example of how changing global trade dynamics are influencing procurement and supply chain strategies. The United Kingdom's departure from the European Union has created new challenges for businesses engaged in cross-border trade between the UK and EU countries. Companies must now navigate new customs procedures, tariffs, and regulatory frameworks, which has increased the complexity of managing supply chains in Europe. As a result, businesses are rethinking their sourcing strategies, considering options for nearshoring or reshoring, and exploring ways to build greater supply chain resilience in response to the uncertainty created by Brexit.

Technology is also playing a significant role in shaping the future of global trade. The rise of the digital economy is driving the need for supply chains to become more agile, data-driven, and technology-enabled. Advancements in technologies such as artificial intelligence, blockchain, and the Internet of Things (IoT) are enabling companies to track goods in real-time, optimize shipping routes, and enhance visibility across borders. These technologies are making it easier for businesses to engage in international trade, even as they face increasing complexity due to regulatory requirements, tariffs, and customs procedures.

In conclusion, evolving global trade dynamics are having a profound impact on procurement and supply chain management. Companies must navigate a more complex, unpredictable global landscape, shaped by regional trade agreements, protectionist policies, and technological advancements. To succeed in this new environment, organizations must adapt their procurement and supply chain strategies to leverage new opportunities, mitigate risks, and enhance resilience. By embracing digital technologies, building more flexible and localized supply chains, and staying informed about geopolitical developments, businesses can position themselves for long-term success in the global marketplace.

Predictions for the Next Decade in Procurement and Supply Chain Management

The landscape of procurement and supply chain management is evolving at an unprecedented pace, driven by a combination of technological advancements, changing global trade dynamics, and shifting consumer expectations. As we look ahead to the next decade, several key trends and predictions are likely to shape the future of this field. These predictions offer a glimpse into how procurement and supply chain professionals will need to adapt to thrive in an increasingly complex, technology-driven environment.

Increased Adoption of Advanced Technologies

One of the most significant predictions for the next decade is the continued and accelerated adoption of advanced technologies across procurement and supply chains. Automation, artificial intelligence (AI), machine learning (ML), blockchain, and the Internet of Things (IoT) will become central to the way organizations manage their supply chains. These technologies will revolutionize how businesses plan, execute, and optimize procurement and logistics activities.

Automation will expand beyond simple, repetitive tasks and will increasingly play a role in strategic decision-making. AI and ML will enable more sophisticated demand forecasting, risk management, and supplier performance evaluation. Predictive analytics will empower organizations to anticipate market shifts, identify supply chain disruptions before they occur, and optimize procurement processes with unprecedented accuracy. Meanwhile, blockchain will play a critical role in enhancing transparency, improving traceability, and ensuring the security of transactions across global supply chains.

The IoT will continue to provide valuable real-time data from every stage of the supply chain, offering unprecedented visibility into inventory, shipment status, and equipment performance. This data, when analyzed with AI-powered systems, will help companies make more informed decisions, optimize operations, and improve customer service. By 2030, it is predicted that supply chains will be largely autonomous, with minimal human intervention needed for day-to-day operations.

Shift Towards Sustainability and Circular Supply Chains

The next decade will witness an intensifying focus on sustainability in procurement and supply chain management. As environmental concerns continue to rise, organizations will be under increasing pressure to adopt green practices and ensure that their supply chains are sustainable. This shift is not just driven by regulatory requirements, but also by growing consumer demand for eco-friendly products and services.

Sustainability will become a key performance metric for procurement and supply chain professionals. Companies will prioritize sourcing from suppliers that adhere to environmentally friendly practices, reduce waste, and minimize their carbon footprint. This will include increasing the use of renewable energy, reducing packaging waste, and utilizing sustainable raw materials. Companies will also be required to report on their sustainability efforts more transparently, making sustainability a cornerstone of their brand identity.

Moreover, the concept of circular supply chains will gain significant traction. In a circular supply chain, products are designed for reuse, repair, and recycling, rather than for disposal. Companies will look for ways to close the loop on product life cycles, using materials that can be repurposed and reducing waste in the process. By 2030, circular supply chains will be common practice in many industries, driven by consumer demand for sustainable goods and stricter environmental regulations.

Resilience and Risk Management at the Forefront

The COVID-19 pandemic highlighted the vulnerabilities in global supply chains, and in response, businesses are increasingly prioritizing resilience in their supply chain strategies. The next decade will see a marked shift toward building more resilient and adaptable supply chains that can withstand disruptions caused by pandemics, natural disasters, geopolitical tensions, and other unexpected events.

Risk management will become an integral part of every procurement and supply chain strategy. Companies will invest in technologies and processes that allow them to monitor and mitigate risks in real-time. Scenario planning, risk assessments, and the development of contingency plans will be standard practice. The focus will shift from cost efficiency to a more balanced approach that also considers the ability to quickly adapt to changes and disruptions.

Diversification of suppliers and geographic regions will also be a key strategy for risk mitigation. Companies will seek to avoid over-reliance on a single supplier or region, as was the case with China during the pandemic. By sourcing from multiple suppliers and regions, companies can reduce their exposure to geopolitical and economic risks, ensuring the continuity of their operations.

The Rise of Digital Trade and E-Commerce

As digital transformation continues to accelerate, the global supply chain will increasingly rely on digital trade platforms. E-commerce and digital marketplaces will expand their reach, transforming procurement from a process that happens primarily through traditional methods to one that is predominantly digital.

E-commerce giants like Amazon and Alibaba will continue to expand their influence on global supply chains, while new digital platforms will emerge to support B2B transactions, enabling companies to connect directly with suppliers, manufacturers, and logistics providers. Blockchain and smart contracts will play an increasingly important role in facilitating secure, automated transactions across digital platforms.

By 2030, digital trade will be the norm, with businesses relying on advanced e-commerce platforms and digital tools to source materials, manage procurement, and coordinate logistics. The rise of digital trade will also support the trend of regionalization, enabling companies to access suppliers and customers across the globe more easily while maintaining localized operations.

Talent and Skills Development for the Future

As technology continues to reshape procurement and supply chain management, the demand for highly skilled professionals will grow. The next decade will see a significant evolution in the skill sets required by procurement and supply chain leaders. While traditional skills such as negotiation, supplier relationship management, and cost analysis will remain important, there will be an increased emphasis on data analysis, technology management, and strategic thinking.

Procurement and supply chain professionals will need to be adept at managing complex, technology-driven environments and leveraging data analytics to make informed decisions. Those who can understand and implement AI, machine learning, and automation tools will be in high demand. Additionally, professionals will need to develop strong collaboration and communication skills, as cross-functional teamwork will become increasingly vital to the success of supply chain operations.

Furthermore, the next decade will see an increased focus on diversity, equity, and inclusion in the procurement and supply chain sectors. Companies will invest in programs to attract diverse talent, fostering a more inclusive workforce that can bring new perspectives to problem-solving and innovation. The push for diversity will be especially important as supply chains become more global and multicultural.

Global Supply Chain Integration

In the coming decade, the trend of global supply chain integration will continue, albeit with a greater focus on flexibility and adaptability. While regionalization and localization will play a larger role, companies will still operate in a global market and seek suppliers and customers worldwide. As technology advances, businesses will be able to manage and integrate supply chains across different continents seamlessly, using real-time data and advanced analytics to ensure smooth operations.

Global trade dynamics will continue to be shaped by evolving trade agreements, regulatory changes, and shifting political landscapes. Companies will need to remain agile, continuously monitoring these changes and adapting their supply chain strategies accordingly. Collaboration between governments, businesses, and trade organizations will be essential in creating an environment that supports efficient global trade, while also addressing concerns such as sustainability, security, and labor standards.

The next decade promises to be a period of significant transformation for procurement and supply chain management. Advances in technology, the rise of digital trade, the focus on sustainability, and the need for resilience will reshape how organizations manage their supply chains. As these trends unfold, procurement and supply chain professionals will need to embrace innovation, invest in new technologies, and develop the skills necessary to navigate an increasingly complex and dynamic global landscape. The companies that can successfully adapt to these changes will not only enhance their competitive edge but will also contribute to the creation of more efficient, sustainable, and resilient supply chains for the future.

Conclusion

As we conclude this exploration into the future of procurement and supply chain management, it is essential to reflect on the key lessons learned throughout the book. The next decade promises to bring immense opportunities, challenges, and transformations to the field, demanding professionals to adapt and innovate at an unprecedented pace. Understanding these shifts and aligning strategies effectively will be crucial to achieving long-term success.

Recap of Key Lessons

One of the most profound lessons is the crucial role technology will play in shaping the future of supply chains. The rise of automation, artificial intelligence, machine learning, blockchain, and the Internet of Things will continue to redefine how procurement and supply chain activities are conducted. Embracing these technologies is not optional but necessary for staying competitive and agile in a rapidly evolving environment. Whether it's predictive analytics for demand forecasting, blockchain for enhanced transparency, or IoT for real-time data-driven decisions, the ability to harness these tools will determine the success of future supply chain strategies.

Sustainability has also emerged as a non-negotiable element of modern supply chain management. From reducing carbon footprints to adopting circular supply chain concepts, organizations will be expected to adopt greener practices. This shift is not only driven by regulatory pressures but by the increasing demand from consumers and stakeholders for businesses to demonstrate environmental and social responsibility. Sustainable procurement and supply chain models will not only align with global efforts to combat climate change but also create a competitive advantage by catering to a conscientious consumer base.

Another key takeaway is the importance of supply chain resilience. The disruptions caused by global events like the COVID-19 pandemic have highlighted the vulnerability of many supply chains. The need for flexibility, adaptability, and robust risk management strategies has never been more evident. The next decade will require businesses to prepare for the unexpected by building agile, resilient supply chains that can withstand a range of global disruptions, from pandemics to geopolitical instability.

In addition to technological advancements and resilience, strategic collaboration and leadership will become even more critical. Supply chains are no longer isolated entities; they are part of a broader ecosystem that requires cross-functional collaboration. Procurement professionals, supply chain managers, and other key stakeholders must work together to align objectives, share insights, and tackle challenges. As such, leadership will play a pivotal role in fostering a culture of collaboration, innovation, and continuous improvement.

Call to Action for Professionals to Apply Strategies Effectively

As procurement and supply chain professionals, it is imperative to take these lessons and apply them strategically within your organizations. The future of supply chain management will be defined by those who can leverage emerging technologies, embrace sustainability, and develop resilient systems. It is not enough to simply understand these concepts; professionals must take proactive steps to implement them in day-to-day operations.

For technology, the call to action is clear: integrate advanced tools and data analytics into your procurement and supply chain processes. Begin by assessing your current systems and identifying opportunities for automation and data-driven decision-making. Embrace tools such as AI and blockchain to enhance operational efficiency, reduce costs, and improve transparency.

On the sustainability front, professionals should work towards integrating green procurement strategies and circular supply chain practices. Start by evaluating your supplier network and ensuring they align with your environmental goals. Set clear, measurable sustainability targets, and actively collaborate with suppliers and customers to create more sustainable supply chain practices.

In terms of resilience, organizations must shift from a focus solely on efficiency to one that also prioritizes adaptability and risk mitigation. Develop robust risk management frameworks and regularly conduct scenario planning exercises to identify potential vulnerabilities. Diversify your supplier base and geographic sourcing to mitigate the impact of disruptions, and implement contingency plans that enable a quick response to unforeseen events.

Finally, as the procurement and supply chain landscape becomes more interconnected, developing strong leadership and collaborative skills will be critical. Encourage cross-departmental communication and collaboration, and foster a culture of innovation. Leaders in procurement and supply chain management should inspire their teams to embrace change and pursue continuous improvement at every level.

In conclusion, the future of procurement and supply chain management is ripe with opportunity, but it will require professionals to be forward-thinking, adaptable, and willing to invest in new technologies and strategies. By embracing these changes and acting decisively, procurement and supply chain leaders can not only position themselves for success but also contribute to the creation of more efficient, sustainable, and resilient global supply chains. The time to act is now – the future is already taking shape, and those who lead the charge will shape it for the better.

Additional Resources

To further enhance your understanding and application of the concepts discussed in this book, we have provided a set of valuable resources. These resources will help expand your knowledge, guide your implementation efforts, and provide you with practical tools and templates to integrate into your procurement and supply chain operations. Whether you're a beginner or an experienced professional, these materials will support your growth and foster continuous improvement in your work.

Glossary of Key Terms

Procurement: The process of acquiring goods, services, or works from external sources through a tendering or purchasing process.

Supply Chain: A network of organizations, people, activities, information, and resources involved in moving a product or service from supplier to customer.

Strategic Sourcing: The process of analyzing an organization's procurement needs and finding the best suppliers to fulfill those needs, focusing on long-term relationships and value creation.

Total Cost of Ownership (TCO): A comprehensive assessment of all direct and indirect costs associated with acquiring, using, and maintaining a product or service throughout its lifecycle.

Lean Supply Chain: A supply chain that focuses on minimizing waste, optimizing resources, and improving efficiency to deliver maximum value to customers.

Agile Supply Chain: A supply chain designed to be highly flexible and responsive to changes in demand and market conditions, focusing on speed and adaptability.

Risk Management: The identification, assessment, and prioritization of risks followed by the application of resources to minimize, monitor, and control the probability or impact of negative events.

Supplier Relationship Management (SRM): The management of a company's interactions with current and potential suppliers, aimed at fostering long-term, mutually beneficial relationships.

Just-in-Time (JIT): A strategy that aligns production schedules with demand, aiming to reduce inventory costs and increase operational efficiency.

ERP (Enterprise Resource Planning): A software system used to manage and integrate core business processes, including procurement, supply chain management, inventory, finance, and human resources.

Blockchain: A distributed ledger technology that records transactions in a secure and transparent way, with applications in supply chain management for tracking products and verifying authenticity.

Circular Supply Chain: A supply chain model that focuses on minimizing waste by reusing, recycling, and refurbishing products, aiming for a closed-loop system where resources are continually cycled back into production.

Collaborative Forecasting: A process where organizations work together, sharing data and insights, to create more accurate demand forecasts that improve supply chain coordination.

Cross-docking: A logistics practice where products are received at a warehouse or distribution center and immediately shipped out to their next destination without being stored.

Vendor-Managed Inventory (VMI): A supply chain model where the supplier manages the inventory levels of their products at the customer's location, ensuring optimal stock levels and reducing stockouts.

Templates for Procurement and Supply Chain Management

Procurement Strategy Template: A comprehensive framework for defining procurement goals, objectives, and strategies, aligning them with organizational goals and operational needs.

Supplier Evaluation Scorecard: A tool for assessing and scoring potential suppliers based on criteria such as cost, quality, delivery, and innovation.

Request for Proposal (RFP) Template: A standardized document used to solicit proposals from suppliers, outlining the organization's needs, expectations, and evaluation criteria.

Procurement Budget Template: A detailed tool for tracking procurement expenses, setting budget limits, and ensuring that procurement activities stay within financial constraints.

Risk Management Plan Template: A guide to identifying potential risks in the supply chain, evaluating their likelihood and impact, and creating mitigation strategies.

Supply Chain Mapping Template: A tool for visualizing the supply chain from raw materials to finished products, identifying key stakeholders, processes, and potential bottlenecks.

Inventory Management Template: A tool for tracking inventory levels, reorder points, lead times, and safety stock to optimize stock management.

Supplier Performance Management Template: A tool to assess and track supplier performance over time, measuring key metrics such as on-time delivery, quality, and compliance.

Demand Forecasting Template: A tool that helps predict future demand based on historical sales data, market trends, and seasonality.

Contract Management Template: A template for drafting, reviewing, and tracking procurement contracts, ensuring compliance and proper documentation throughout the contract lifecycle.

Recommended Reading and References

"The Procurement and Supply Manager's Desk Reference" by Fred Sollish and John Semanik
This comprehensive guide covers every aspect of procurement and supply chain management, from basic principles to advanced strategic approaches. It is an excellent resource for professionals looking to enhance their expertise.

"Supply Chain Management: Strategy, Planning, and Operation" by Sunil Chopra and Peter Meindl
A highly recommended textbook for understanding the core principles and strategies in supply chain management. It covers topics like network design, logistics, inventory management, and procurement in great depth.

"Lean Supply Chain and Logistics Management" by Paul Myerson
This book offers valuable insights into lean principles and how they can be applied to improve the efficiency and performance

of the supply chain. It provides practical strategies for reducing waste and increasing value for customers.

"The Toyota Way: 14 Management Principles from the World's Greatest Manufacturer" by Jeffrey K. Liker
A classic text that explores the principles behind Toyota's success in manufacturing and supply chain management. The book delves into lean principles, continuous improvement, and how they can be applied in various industries.

"Supply Chain Risk Management: Minimizing Disruptions in Global Sourcing" by Robert J. Trent
This book offers practical approaches for managing risk in global supply chains. It covers strategies for identifying, assessing, and mitigating supply chain risks, particularly in complex global sourcing environments.

"Strategic Sourcing and Category Management: Lessons Learned in Global Procurement" by Mark P. R. McCormack
A must-read for those in procurement roles, this book offers practical advice and real-world lessons on strategic sourcing and category management. It covers topics like supplier relationship management, negotiations, and cost control.

"The Handbook of Logistics and Distribution Management" by Alan Rushton, Phil Croucher, and Peter Baker
This is a comprehensive reference guide for logistics professionals. It covers everything from inventory management to transportation, warehousing, and distribution strategies.

"Blockchain and the Supply Chain: Concepts, Strategies and Practical Applications" by K. N. S. Yadav
For professionals interested in the intersection of blockchain technology and supply chain management, this book provides

an in-depth look at how blockchain can be applied to enhance supply chain transparency, traceability, and efficiency.

"Sustainable Supply Chains: A Research-Based Textbook on Operations and Strategy" by Olli-Pekka Hilmola, Pasi Lautala, and Ari-Pekka Henttonen
A deep dive into sustainable supply chain practices, this book explores green logistics, environmental impact assessments, and the integration of sustainability into supply chain management.

"The Lean Supply Chain: Managing the Challenge at Tesco" by Barry Evans and Robert Mason
This book offers a practical case study of Tesco's lean supply chain transformation. It covers the implementation of lean principles, challenges faced, and lessons learned, providing valuable insights for other organizations.

These readings will equip procurement and supply chain professionals with the knowledge to address the complexities of modern supply chains, implement best practices, and stay ahead in an ever-evolving field. By integrating these resources into your professional development, you can continually refine your strategies and drive greater efficiency, sustainability, and resilience in your organization's procurement and supply chain operations.

Appendix

This appendix includes a variety of practical resources designed to assist procurement and supply chain professionals in the implementation and management of best practices. The following materials provide valuable tools for enhancing procurement strategies, evaluating suppliers, and learning from real-world supply chain transformations. These resources can be used as references, templates, or case studies to guide decision-making and continuous improvement in supply chain and procurement management.

Sample Procurement Policies

A well-structured procurement policy is essential to ensure that procurement activities are conducted ethically, efficiently, and in alignment with organizational goals. Below is a sample procurement policy outline that organizations can adapt to fit their unique needs.

Procurement Policy Framework:

Introduction and Purpose

The purpose of this procurement policy is to define the guidelines for acquiring goods, services, and works in a manner that ensures transparency, fairness, and compliance with legal and organizational requirements.

It aims to ensure that procurement is carried out in a way that maximizes value for money, reduces risk, and supports sustainability.

Scope and Applicability

This policy applies to all departments and functions involved in the procurement process, including purchasing, tendering, supplier selection, and contract management.

It covers the procurement of all goods, services, and works, both domestic and international.

Procurement Procedures

Supplier Selection: Procurement will be conducted through competitive bidding processes such as Requests for Quotation (RFQ), Requests for Proposal (RFP), or Invitations to Tender (ITT).

Contract Management: All procurement contracts must be documented and include terms and conditions that outline the responsibilities of both parties, including performance, payment terms, and dispute resolution procedures.

Ethical Standards: All procurement activities must adhere to ethical standards, including anti-corruption policies, fair competition, and social responsibility.

Budgeting and Approval Process

Procurement activities must be within the budgetary constraints set by the organization. All procurement decisions must be approved by designated financial authorities.

Prior to procurement, a budget proposal must be submitted, outlining the anticipated costs and justifications.

Sustainability and Environmental Considerations

Procurement decisions must consider the environmental impact of purchased goods and services, prioritizing green procurement practices and sustainable sourcing where possible.

Conflict of Interest and Transparency

All procurement officers must disclose any potential conflicts of interest. Procurement decisions must be made based on objective criteria and should be transparent to ensure accountability.

Compliance and Auditing

The procurement process will be regularly audited to ensure compliance with internal policies and external regulations.

Training and Development

Procurement staff will undergo regular training to stay updated on industry trends, regulatory changes, and best practices in procurement management.

Checklist for Supplier Evaluations

Supplier evaluation is critical to ensuring that the right suppliers are selected to meet organizational needs. The following checklist provides a comprehensive set of criteria to evaluate potential suppliers in an objective and systematic manner.

Supplier Evaluation Checklist:

Supplier Information and Company Background

Legal name, address, and contact details.

Length of time in business.

Reputation and experience in the industry.

Financial Stability

Review of financial statements (profit and loss, balance sheet).

Credit rating or history of timely payments.

Adequate cash flow and the ability to scale operations.

Quality Assurance

Does the supplier have ISO certifications or other industry-recognized quality standards?

Evidence of quality control measures and procedures.

Historical performance related to product defects, returns, and complaints.

Delivery and Lead Time

Supplier's ability to meet required delivery schedules.

Flexibility to handle rush orders or changes in order volumes.

On-time delivery performance history.

Pricing and Cost Competitiveness

Comparative pricing with other suppliers in the market.

Payment terms and discounts offered for bulk orders or early payments.

Hidden costs (shipping, handling, customs duties, etc.).

Capacity and Capability

Supplier's ability to meet demand, both currently and in the future.

Availability of resources, including labor, equipment, and technology.

Scalability of production or services.

Compliance and Certifications

Compliance with industry standards, regulations, and legal requirements (e.g., environmental, labor, safety).

Certifications relevant to your industry (e.g., ISO, GMP, Fair Trade).

Customer Service and Support

Responsiveness and communication channels.

Availability of after-sales support or technical assistance.

Return policies and warranty conditions.

Innovation and Continuous Improvement

Supplier's commitment to research and development.

History of implementing process improvements or introducing new products.

Willingness to engage in joint ventures or collaborative innovation efforts.

Sustainability Practices

Supplier's commitment to sustainable practices, such as energy conservation, waste reduction, and responsible sourcing.

Environmental certifications, such as ISO 14001.

Social responsibility initiatives, such as fair labor practices and community involvement.

Case Studies of Successful Supply Chain Transformations

Case studies provide valuable lessons on how companies can successfully implement supply chain transformation strategies. These real-world examples demonstrate how organizations can overcome challenges, optimize operations, and achieve significant business improvements.

Case Study 1: Ford's Global Supply Chain Transformation

Ford Motor Company's global supply chain transformation focused on reducing lead times, improving supplier relationships, and enhancing overall operational efficiency. The company implemented a robust supplier integration program, encouraging suppliers to share real-time inventory data and collaborate on demand forecasting. This transparency enabled Ford to streamline its procurement processes, reduce inventory levels, and achieve cost savings.

By implementing a more synchronized approach to procurement, Ford was able to improve the reliability of its supply chain, enhance product quality, and meet consumer demands more effectively. Ford's supply chain transformation also included the adoption of new technologies, such as cloud-based platforms and advanced data analytics, to improve decision-making and optimize the end-to-end supply chain process.

Key Takeaways:

> Supplier collaboration and integration are critical for reducing lead times and improving supply chain efficiency.

> Leveraging technology, such as cloud computing and data analytics, can provide greater visibility and control over supply chain operations.

> Strategic sourcing and improved forecasting are vital for maintaining product availability and meeting market demands.

Case Study 2: Unilever's Sustainable Supply Chain Practices

Unilever, a global consumer goods company, embarked on a journey to transform its supply chain by focusing on sustainability. Unilever implemented green procurement strategies, which included sourcing raw materials from suppliers who adhere to strict environmental and social standards. The company also integrated sustainability criteria into its supplier evaluation process, ensuring that suppliers met specific environmental and ethical standards.

Unilever's sustainable supply chain practices extended beyond sourcing raw materials. The company also worked to reduce the carbon footprint of its logistics and transportation operations by optimizing routes, reducing packaging waste, and collaborating with logistics providers on sustainable transportation solutions.

The company's commitment to sustainability was not only beneficial for the environment but also resulted in cost savings, improved brand image, and greater consumer loyalty. By adopting a circular supply chain model, Unilever was able to recycle materials and reduce waste, ultimately contributing to long-term profitability.

Key Takeaways:

> A sustainable supply chain is not just beneficial for the environment but also enhances brand reputation and customer loyalty.

> Integrating sustainability into supplier selection and evaluation can drive value for both the organization and its suppliers.

> Circular supply chains, which focus on recycling and reusing materials, are an essential strategy for reducing waste and increasing sustainability.